Summer's Song

& other Essays

By
Don L. Johnson

Library of Congress Control Number: 2005934081

Preface

"If you have remarked errors in me, your superior knowledge must pardon them. Who errs not while perambulating the domain of nature? Who can observe everything with accuracy? Correct me as a friend, and I as a friend will requite with kindness."

Carolus Linnaeus -- 1707-78

The quote is from the Swedish scientist who established the system still used for classifying all manner of plants and animals. His words were entered in my daily journal more than 40 years ago, as a reminder that we are never infallible regarding nature.

But that is the wonder of it. I might have wearied of outdoor explorations decades ago if not for frequent discoveries which delighted my senses and further whetted my curiosity.

It was my good fortune to find a career which enabled me to roam, quite unfettered, from deep jungles to tall mountains. However, it was during hikes along Wisconsin woodland trails, often with notebook in hand, that I found almost daily enjoyment.

An essay sharing those simple pleasures was submitted to the editors of The Milwaukee Sentinel, not long after I had signed on as that newspaper's outdoor writer and columnist in 1962. Somewhat to my surprise, it appeared the next day on the front page, nicely illustrated by a Sentinel artist. Reader response echoed the reception the piece had received from my editors, so that was the first of many such features appearing in the paper during the next two decades.

It was often suggested that I collect my writings into a book, and I routinely answered that I might. However, after 23 eventful years with The Sentinel, I found myself equally busy as a freelance writer, so the project remained "on hold" until recently.

Nonetheless, over the years I continued to take daily walks with my dog, often making notes and taking photos. And I still wrote an occasional essay. Some were published in The Sentinel or elsewhere. Others were simply filed away. A few of those later pieces are included in this collection.

Many of these essays were drawn from the place where I lived from 1964 to 1991. It covered about 10 acres in western Waukesha County, and its varied landscape -- highland and marsh, hardwood hills and tamarack swamp, field and fencerow, seeping spring and rippling creek -- provided unending inspiration. Yet, I have found places equally fascinating virtually everywhere.

Selection of the pieces was a purely subjective process. Hundreds of features and columns had been torn from the daily paper and "filed" in a cardboard cartons labeled *"Essays. Book."*

As I paged through them, I recalled that some had won particular praise or recognition. Others evoked special memories. I chose to include those which met either or both of those tests.

How to organize the material was another puzzle. Because the writings were taken from a span of widely varied years, presenting them in chronological sequence did not have the orderly appearance one might expect. Springtime was early or tardy, summers were wet or dry, fall colors were muted or bright; winter was mild or bitter. Wisconsin weather being what it is, mid-April could be far different from one year to the next.

Other differences are evident. For example, the essays tell of summers filled with bluebirds; others when they were rare. And they record their gradual return.

Wood ducks and eagles and pileated woodpeckers are among other species which have made comebacks during the decades described, while numbers of meadowlarks, bobolinks, black ducks and butterflies have dwindled.

In some ways, Wisconsin seems wilder than when the first essays in this book were written. Timber wolves and elk have returned. Wild turkeys now flourish. Coyotes roam everywhere and black bears have vastly expanded their range. But at the same time, woodcock coverts have been converted into strip malls and golf courses and subdivisions.

So in the end, it was decided to keep the chronology -- first by month and day; then by year. And if environmental changes are thereby brought to the readers' attention, that is all to the good.

Some may think it strange that this book begins in July rather than January. But why not? Books, like lives, can begin in at any month. And besides, it seemed appropriate to begin with the title piece -- a personal favorite, and one which brought special praise from the editor of an eastern seaboard newspaper.

The editor was on a trip, with a stopover in Milwaukee, when he picked up a copy of The Sentinel and read the "Summer's Song" essay. Before leaving town, he penned a note to my boss, declaring the piece an example of "the literature of journalism."

Harvey Schwandner, then executive editor of The Sentinel, had a reputation as a stern taskmaster, so it was with some trepidation that I answered a summons to his office. Looking dour, he shoved the note across his desk and told me to read it. Then he smiled and gave me a raise.

Mind you now, this book is not meant to be read from cover to cover in one sitting. Rather, its pages are to be turned to whatever season is appropriate to the time and mood. That way, we will be walking together.

While on the subject of walking companions, it is fitting, I think, to dedicate these pages to the dogs which have shared life's trails with me. Especially Dash, Chips and Brighton. Each in turn accompanied me on most of the treks described herein.

And finally, special thanks to Keith Spore, former Milwaukee Sentinel editor and president of Journal Communications, Inc., for permission to use previously published materials.

Table of Contents

November

December

January

February

March

April

May

June

JULY

SUMMER SONG

Summer is humming her sleepy tune again. The lazy bumbling of bees in golden sweet clover and purple vetch. The whispering rustle of dragonfly wings.

It is a soft song that summer sings. It is of fading phlox and empty nests and spittlebugs. Of lupine and campion and spiderwort, goatsbeard, hawkweed, nightshade and rose.

The notes tell of brown buttons of acorns, of shiny green fruit in cherry trees, of turtle eggs stirring in warm earth. And of summers long gone.

For when sunbeams have lapped the dew, when birds have hushed and leaves droop in the hazy heat, then summer drones to other days:

So hum a lullaby summer, while we drowse and dream. Remembering the scent of new-mown hay and tickle of the stubble on calloused toes. Quail whistling, and fresh-caught crawdads clattering in a pail. And jeweled beetles, slithering snakes, and butterflies, bib overalls and berries.

Do barefoot boys still listen to your tunes?

Sing summer, of the taste of milk still foamy and warm, and of the whir of the cream separator when the big crank was turned. Let me hear that score once more.

Summer, sing of pale butter churned in a jar, melting on fresh, crusty bread. And of tart-smelling kettles of bubbling jellies and jams. And of the whiskery rasp of barley being gathered into shocks.

Louder notes then, summer, to the tempo of the treadle as a grindstone shrills at a scythe, of pump handles squealing and stove lids clanging and swallows twittering from the barn beams. shocks. You remember. You were there.

Summer, recall those old tunes for us again. We each have our own lyrics. Just hum to me while I remember mine.

(07/02/68)

THE HEX

Wautoma, Wis. -- A deer, its russet summer coat as bright as barn paint against the lush greenery, watched curiously as I started down the marshy path. The sun, settling in its bed, yawned from a hazy horizon.

It was hot. Sticky. Rivulets of sweat were already trickling within my waders. Mosquitoes were whining shrill welcomes in my ears.

Of all the madness which is excused as sport, this may be the worst. I had been hexed. The spell impelling me down that trail is known as "the hex hatch." It is a phenomenon which stirs trout -- and trouters -- to frenzy. Fortunately, it all happens after dark when sane people can't see us. Otherwise, instead of fishing vests we'd all be wearing white coats with very long sleeves.

"Will you be up on the White River tonight?" Royce Dam had asked when we met on a downtown Milwaukee sidewalk that very morning. "A heavy hex hatch is due," he promised.

Royce is a guru of flyfishers, a master fly tyer and caster whose floppy Stetson and patched waders are known from the fabled Brule to Bluebottle Creek.

"I'm thinking about it, but don't wait for me if I don't show up," I'd answered.

"Are you going to hit the hex hatch tonight?" Ned Vespa had asked later, as we met in the company cafeteria for lunch.

"I'm figuring on it," I'd said, obviously weakening.

Ned is another member of the cult. He uses the Orvis catalog for a checklist when packing to go fishing. He also makes his own rods.

12

Beautifully crafted; light as air.

The sun was sinking fast when I arrived at the river. Parked cars told me that Royce and Ned were already there, along with perhaps a dozen more of the clandestine clan. The hatch would not begin until deep dusk, but it was wise to stake out a stretch of stream before dark. Hurriedly, I pulled on my waders and rigged my rod. I even paused to spray cap and shirt with insect repellent although sure that it would soon be carried away in rivulets of sweat.

Two anglers were wading in the first pool, where the path meets the river.

"Any action yet?"

"No, but tonight should be the night!"

I backtracked and took another trail to a point downstream.

"Is that you Royce?" I asked a fisherman who was standing in shoulder-high weeds across the creek. It was, and Ned was close by. As I waded across to join them, I noticed some Mayflies clinging to branches along the bank.

Mayfly, mind you, is a misnomer for many of the ephemeral creatures so-named. Many of them make their brief, fluttering appearances much earlier or later in the year. The *Hexagenia limbata* usually emerges in late June and is one of the most important insects to anglers (if not to trout) on many Wisconsin streams. Anglers usually see it as a large, yellow-brown or orange-tinted fly with two tails and transparent, cross-veined wings. Trout also see it in other stages,
including the tasty nymphs which bait fishermen call "wigglers".

Mayflies live complicated lives, mostly under water, hidden beneath rocks, gravel or silt. They come in varied hues and sizes and undergo three major transformations, but trout know them in all of their disguises.

They feed on the nymphs along the bottom, or as they rise to the surface. They gulp them again as the ride on the surface, sprouting dusky wings to take flight as "duns". The duns rest on nearby branches, moult a final time and emerge as clear-winged "spinners" (also sometimes called "drakes") which at last take flight to mate.

As the females return to the water to deposit their eggs they offer another banquet for trout. Then, life over, they letter the water as "spent-wings." There's not much nutrition left in spent-wings, but sometimes trout gorge on them too.

Of course, those are all common fly fisher's terms. More scientific types call spinners "imagos" and duns "sub-imagos" and recite litanies of entomological Latin each time a hatch appears. Now that all of that is clear, we come to the hard part: Catching trout,

"We've got a hatch!" I heard Royce say. He was just beyond my sight, upstream. Ned was working a pool below. Trout were making swift, slurping sounds nearby.

Sandhill cranes trumpeted taps in the distance. A bullfrog strummed a lullaby. Fireflies flickered. Flylines swished.

The moon was near full, sparkling on river riffles. For a time there was enough light to see my ivory-colored line and the white Wulff fly. Finally there were only glints of moonlight in deep shadows and I was literally playing it by ear.

A trout was rising repeatedly near the opposite bank. I cast blindly, trying to drop the fly gently and drift it naturally past that spot. I tried again and again. Now there was a blizzard of flies in the air. What chance had my imitation of being taken?

Reacting to a quick twitch on the line, I hooked a lively trout, but it was only a small brown, perhaps eight inches. I shook it off and began casting to a louder slurp upstream. My leader became tangled. I had a small flashlight dangling from a lanyard around my neck. I held the light in my mouth as I tried to untwist the all-but-invisible monofilament. In frustration, I broke off the fly and lost it in the weeds. Mosquitoes swarmed to the light as I struggled to fasten another fly to the tippet. It gets harder every year. You can tell an old fly fisher by his squinty eyes.

"There's a big one working over there," I heard Royce say.

A voice behind him answered, "Yeah, I lost a big one by that bush last night." The trout slurped loudly.

With one of Royce's realistic hex imitations finally attached to my tippet, I began casting, casting, casting to those sounds. No takers. Were the trout taking rising nymphs? Emerging duns? Returning spinners? It was impossible to tell, but the answer was critical. Feeding trout are as selective as they are fickle. You try to match the hatch.

Casting too far, I snagged on the far bank and lost another fly. After another squinty struggle I replaced it with a dun pattern. In the dim beam from my flashlight I could see spent-wings riding the current like fallen confetti. The parade was almost over, The slurping sounds were diminishing. It was nearly 10:30 p. m.

A few casts later I caught and released another brown, not much bigger than the first. Then the river was quiet. Too quiet.

"Well, good luck. I'm hauling out," said the voice behind Royce, fading upstream.

"Me too," I called. It would be after 2 a. m. before I got to bed, and my schedule called for an early start in the morning.

Royce and Ned had decided to quit too. Trekking back to the road with them, I .learned that Ned had caught one small trout while Royce, concentrating on that big one, had struck out.

Two other fishermen were loading up in the parking area. One of them showed us a beautiful brown trout, maybe four pounds.

"There was too much moon tonight," Royce said. "And the hatch was really too heavy for good fishing."

"I got this one before the hatch started," the fisherman said, nodding agreement.

I was wondering if I would ever know anything for sure about this trout fishing.

"Are you going to try to hit the hatch on the Brule?" Royce asked, turning to me.

"Maybe, but don't wait for me," I said.

(07/02/83)

A LONE BLUEBIRD

There's an old saying that "one swallow does not a summer make."
Aristophanes said that some 2,400 years ago, and it has since been repeated by Aristotle and a long list of other pundits. So maybe it's true.

But I know for sure that one bluebird does.

One bird with plumage that reflects the dazzling sky, with breast like cottony cloud and rosy sunset, has made summer a reality out our way.

Yes, there have been other signs -- chipmunks stuffing their cheeks with mulberries, pale roses and purple thistles; fireflies sparking over the marsh -- but summer's arrival was affirmed by a few cheery notes greeting me in the garden on a dew-drenched morning:

"Cheer, cheerful charmer!" they seemed to say.

I straightened from weed-pulling and looked around.

"Cheer--chirr-chirr..." The songster said, fluttering down from a nearby fencepost. He cocked his head and gave me a cordial look. His arrival was welcome, but it came with many questions: Where was this bird in early spring, when a house was kept ready for his arrival? Where was his mate? And if he had none, why? Was there some bond which had brought him back to us? Was it nostalgia? Loneliness?

Now, as I work outside, the bluebird often follows. He flies off to catch a bug; then returns to tell me about it. As I work in the garage, he sits on a window sill and watches. Sometimes too, he peers through the house windows.

I've seen him perched on the car parked in the driveway. He clings to the sideview mirror. Is it the reflection which holds him?

"He must have been somebody's pet," my wife has guessed.

Perhaps so. However, I believe that he is one of scores of bluebirds which once lived around our country home. He is a lone, and lonely, survivor of some yet unknown disaster.

For many years, at least two pairs of bluebirds nested in the houses we provided for them. Each pair usually raised two broods annually, and the family gatherings before their autumn flights were something to behold.

Three springs ago, none returned. Some calamity had befallen bluebirds over the winter. Not only our neighborhood, but the entire Midwest was affected. I traveled widely, but rarely heard a bluebird's song.

Again last spring, there were no bluebirds to challenge the tree swallows for housing at our place. However, as summer arrived, a single male appeared. He stayed almost constantly within sight and sound of our house. We never saw a female.

Then, on a brisk morning last October, nine bluebirds stopped in for a brief visit. Surely they were parents and young. And when they were gone, so was our special friend. So had he a family after all, hidden somewhere nearby? I doubted that such a thing could escape my notice.

And now he is back. The same bird, certainly. The mystery is renewed.

Swallows? They returned in welcome numbers again this spring. These days they are busy trying to quiet the clamor of their hungry young. The parent birds swoop threateningly at our approach, a sure

18

sign that fledglings are almost ready to try their wings. We have enough swallows then, to make the season a certainty.

But the real clincher is perched on our weather vane as I scribble these notes. He wears no identifying band; bears no special marks, but I think we know his name.

Just call him Summer.

(07/10/80)

HOT FOR TROUT

It was hot. Haze was draped over the distant water like a veil over shimmering stain.

It was quiet. There was only that faint hum, as though one can hear the deep whirring of the earth on its axis.

The flies had stopped buzzing. Even the leech fastened to my boot had stopped writhing. It was one of those moments when time stops. It was like a movie film which halts, projecting the same still scene on the screen for long seconds. You see details in the picture then that would escape you while the reel is turning.

What I saw was a trout. It appeared suddenly in the foreground. I don't mean it swam into view. Nothing moved. It simply materialized as I peered into the beaver pond. First there was just the suggestion of a line, then a shadow which abruptly took on form and substance. If I needed more proof that the heat was affecting me, the clincher was the size of the fish. Brook trout do not grow that big any more. Not where I fish, anyway.

I had taken a break from a long drive, and made the sweltering hike from the road simply to visit a favorite scene. I had pictured the deep shade along the pond bank and yearned for the feel of cool water rising around my boots. The water would likely be too low, and anyway, midday was a poor time to try for trout. So it was more habit than hope that prompted me take the flyrod.

But now, in slow motion, I stripped line from the reel. There already was a No. 8 muddler minnow tied to the tippet. It was as well worth a try as anything.

The trout was in a little bay where wind and current had assembled the pond's flotsam. The surface was criss-crossed with windfallen branches and sticks peeled by beaver teeth. Those jumbled jackstraws framed small windows of open water -- more like pieces of broken glass. The trout lazed under there in the shade. It must have been dozing, for my approach had not been particularly cautious.

Mentally, I fished the spot from every angle. Then I began gently rolling the fly to the fringed of the tangle, trying to lure the trout from its lair. It paid no attention. In growing desperation, I waded nearer, oozing my feet through the bottom mud until I could dapple the fly almost directly above the fish. The trout rose a few inches, its tail waving slowly. Then it was gone. I do not mean it swam away. It simply disappeared.

I tried casting to other parts of the pond. Nothing. My fly snagged and I snapped it off. A deer fly bit my wrist. My watch said that 40 minutes had passed. Time was racing to make up for that brief interlude with the trout. I wound up my line and started back to the road.

But in a dream last night, I danced a fly lightly over that pond and a big trout slurped it down. That's how it will be the next time -- or maybe the time after that. For I will go back, and back again. And that is how a fish hooks a man.

(07/11/72)

CO-EXISTING WITH SWALLOWS

Now there are mint-scented dawns sparkling with dew. Now ranks of loosestrife march through the marsh, unfurling purple flags. Iridescent dragonflies patrol the creek. Silver minnows hover in the current.

Caterpillars and polliwogs; butterflies and spotted frogs. Summer is keeping the promises of spring.

New arrivals to our country home this year were barn swallows, swift, sleek birds whose aerobatics are a wonder to watch. However, they have been a mixed blessing. The trouble is, they are trying to evict us.

In the backyard, in the garden, anywhere within their sight, we've become targets of hair-raising attacks. Shrieking threats, the birds swoop unerringly within an inch of one's scalp. Surely they wouldn't risk injury by actually striking us, but that sudden rush of wings is unnerving, especially when it comes from behind when one is weeding the rutabagas.

And because their nest is just above a living room window, their fussing and cussing continues even when I'm reading in my favorite chair. The swallows repeat their insults, diving just outside the screen, each time we enter the room. Meanwhile, their frog-faced young peer over the edge of the nest, impatient for their next meal.

That nest is another of nature's marvels. Begun in frantic haste in late May, it wasn't completed until two weeks later. While attempting to fasten a foundation to the vertical brick wall, the swallows failed a

22

hundred times. Pellets of mud littered the window sill below. It seemed that the local mud was too sandy to adhere. But at last some suitable material was found, and, with grass woven in for reinforcement, a cup of clay took shape just under the eave. Eggs appeared on the feathery lining of the nest, even before the last course of mud were placed.

Although tree swallows are regular summer residents, this was the first pair of barn swallows to settle on our place. Why they chose a spot with so many problems, and why they nested so late (at a time when a second brood might normally be started) only they might know.

Their wildness is a puzzle too. The barn swallows of my boyhood nested on low beams, watching unconcerned while the milking and other chores were being done. Their main worries were the all-knowing barn cats, which waited patiently as young swallows prepared to bail out.

Despite the attitude of the new tenants, there are benefits to having swallows under the eaves. Like their tree-dwelling kin, they swoop and soar from dawn to dusk, collecting all manner of airborne insects.

Mosquitoes and deer flies are few. Even wasps, which usually nest under our eaves, are absent this summer. Although our home is at the edge of a woods, and overlooks a marsh, the birds keep insect problems to a minimum. Big city backyards have more bugs than ours.

Those feisty swallows are tolerant of robins, flickers, orioles, redwings, thrashers and grosbeaks, all nesting nearby. Neither do they pay any attention to the squirrels, chipmunks and cottontails.

Instead, all of their wrath is aimed at two familiar humans and the resident dog, none of whom has provoked them in any way.

Well, they'll just have to learn to live with us. We're not about to leave.

Not when goldfinches fall like sunbeams to the purple thistles. Not when a wood thrush is piping to the evening and fireflies are sparking across the swamp.

And not when summer says there's more to come, tomorrow.

(07/13/81)

SO LITTLE TIME

There is a moment of silence in midsummer. It is when the night sounds are hushed, just before dawn's luminous vapors swirl over the bogs. Before the sun appears, birdsong begins. Chirping robins are soon answered by chattering wrens and hollow tunes of doves. Quickly then, the woodland world is awake. And hurrying.

Green foliage, sparkling with dew, shines from the shadows. as the sun peers over the horizon. Yellow woodsorrel unfolds its fresh, vinegary-tasting leaves. The volume of birdsong increases. Listen: There is an urgency in the notes.

The truth is, although summer's tempo seems slow and sleepy, it really is a time for haste.

A wood duck hastens a dark, downy brood across the creek's current, the ducklings clustered as tightly as a swarm of bees. The hen must hurry, not only because there is danger where northern pike lurk, but because her hatch was late. There is little time for her young to sprout pinions and build strength for the long fall flight.

In a nearby fallow field, fuzzy little foxes tumble from a den, tussling under the vixen's watchful gaze. Tiring of the game, one stalks a creeping cricket. A pounce and the insect is pinned beneath its forepaws. Mother watches with approval. There is much to learn, and there is little time to spare.

Even flowers must keep a schedule. Many bloom fleetingly, seeding and withering in time to make room for their successors. Feathery caps are replacing the bright-orange flowers of the hawkweeds. Wild geranium blooms have given way to odd-shaped seedpods. Only fuzzy seed cases and browning leaves remain of the blue lupine. Columbines have wilted and phlox wanes.

There is also purposeful haste in the seemingly aimless fluttering of butterflies. Silver-spotted wings of fritillaries are flashing in the clover, and monarchs are busy in the milkweeds. Each butterfly's eggs must be laid at particular times and places to allow for a complex cycle of changes. There is little time to lose.

In the mossy bog a pitcher plant is blooming. Its delicate purple and yellow shadings are no solace to the insects which drowned in the pitcher's inviting pool. Were they in too much haste? Perhaps.

Meanwhile, on still water nearby, a water beetle darts into a group of striders. The frenzied insects skim across the filmy surface, leaping in terror. Even for them, a summer day is no time to doze.

During a simmering afternoon, cicadas shriek at those who would rest. Crows rally to harass a hawk. Squirrels rustle through the hazels, impatient to gather the unripe nuts. All hurrying, hurrying....

And then the sun is plummeting down, gathering speed as it plunges through pink and purple clouds on the horizon. It must hurry back, for summer days must begin early to allow time for all that needs doing.

At last a whippoorwill proclaims that it is bedtime at last. But listen closely: Its lilting call is repeated again and again and again.

It has an urgent sound.

(07/18/63)

SUMMER DAWN

Summer dawns are tranquil times.

Whippoorwills bid farewell to the night. Fireflies flicker away. Stars fade. A dove awakens, a yawn in its haunting song.

Robins chirp briefly. A wren chatters and a redwing trills, just once. A cardinal whistles softly, a mere echo of its exultant voice in spring. A wood thrush pipes a few hesitant notes. A catbird mews.

The sun lays a red carpet across the horizon for the sun. An awed hush falls. And so another summer day begins.

How unlike the dawns of May, when sound swells from every feathered breast. Now we hear nothing from the sandhill cranes and Canada geese which nest nearby. The oriole, the veery; even the exuberant brown thrasher seem strangely silent.

All for good reasons. Mates have been secured; territories established. There are fewer causes for sounding off -- and perhaps better reasons for not announcing one's whereabouts too loudly or often.

Crows, jays and grackles go about their business -- which includes raiding nests -- with uncharacteristic stealth these days. Wisely then, the tanager and ovenbird are loathe to advertise their presence.

But beyond that, the birds are just too busy these days to stop and chatter. There have been eggs to lay and incubate, young to feed and teach. And yes, there are yet nests to be built, for thistles still bloom gaudily in fallow fields.

The goldfinch does not weave its nest until the thistle blossoms have gone to seed. Quickly then, the tiny brown hen will spin a cup from milkweed and other fine fibers. She then will fashion a rim from strands of bark, bind all with caterpillar silk and spider web, and line the hollow with thistledown.

The structure will be so watertight that it may hold rain for hours. However, the hen's wings will serve as an umbrella while her diminutive blue-white eggs or downy chicks are in the nest.

Cattail or milkweed fibers might be substituted for the nest lining, but goldfinches rarely stay where thistles are not found. The little wild canaries relish the thistle's tiny seeds, eating prodigious quantities of them, along with those of ragweed, dandelion, goldenrod, and other "noxious" plants listed by the township's weed commissioner. Their diet is further varied with caterpillars and aphids. also no friends of the farmer. One wonders then, about the wisdom of eradicating thistles and evicting goldfinches.

Although other birds nest earlier than the goldfinch, their parenting is not over. Some, like the duck and pheasant, spend weeks protecting their broods and preparing them for life on their own. Others, whose offspring literally fly from the nest, may raise two or more broods each summer.

The record in my field notes was set by a pair of mourning doves. They began nesting on Feb. 27, 1981, and the first pair of young took wing exactly one month later. Two more eggs were laid immediately and the second brood vacated on April 27. Nesting began anew the nest day, and the third brood flew off on May 30. And then there was the fourth, leaving on June 28.

The nest was vacant for a month. (Whether the doves were taking a break, or were raising a brood elsewhere, I cannot say). They reappeared on July 27, and departed with their fifth brood on August 27.

28

Although mourning doves raise their young just two at a time, (and in nests so small that the chicks face in opposite directions so they'll fit), they are among our most prolific native birds.

So lots of doves are visiting our lawn these days, along with pint-sized rabbits and speckle-breasted young robins.

Squirrels and chipmunks are eyeing the swelling hickory nuts. Catbirds are perched impatiently in the elderberry bushes. They haven't long to wait.

Summer dawns may sound lazy, but things are happening fast these seemingly sleepy days.

(07/18/83)

A SECRET MADNESS

The trail is choked with rank growth, almost shoulder high in places. It is easier to walk in the bordering woods, despite the cold showers of dew brushed from low branches.

Mosquitoes are shrilling around your ears and a deer fly is making nervous touch-and-go landings on the nape of your neck. Rivulets of sweat crawl between your shoulder blades. Your hip boots are already as wet inside as out.

Who would want to take such a hike on a muggy summer morning?

A grouse chick flutters up, flailing the air for a few yards before bumping down. Two others follow. The unseen hen is calling nearby.

The deer fly has now scissored through your skin. You swat, bringing back a hand smeared with blood. The mosquitoes shriek at the scent of it.

Who, in his right mind, would choose to be here?

Beyond the spruce swamp is a clearing where blackberries are ripening. Stopping amid clawing briars to gather a mouthful of the sweet-tart fruit, you note that others have been picking there. A bear cub has left its track where a little creek trickles from the swamp. A woods with a bear in it is always more interesting. However, the probable presence of a sow bear with young makes the berry patch less inviting. So what are you doing there?

Plod on until the murmuring music of spilling water tells you that you are near the pond, and that the beaver dam is still intact. The flyrod in your hand seems to quiver in anticipation.

30

There are those who say that beaver and trout don't mix. They are right, of course. (Except that, somehow, trout and beaver co-existed long before man arrived to do any research on the subject).

Ahead is a young beaver pond, unsilted, cold and deep. The water is dark and still, bordered by brush and littered with flotsam. Branches will snag your fly, you will trip on the tangled bottom as you wade, and the cold water will snatch your breath like a punch in the belly. What could be worth all that?

Slowly now, quietly, strip line from the reel. Twenty feet is enough. Mend it out on the water in lazy curves. Then, lacking room for a backcast, you raise the rod past vertical, then whip it downward to roll the line across the water like a hoop.

A little black gnat alights out there at the end of the leader. Imagine now that you are that gnat, struggling to become airborne. A shadow rises from the deep, hovers under the fly; then surfaces in a sudden swirl. Your timing must be off. You missed setting the hook. Your line limply rides the widening ripples from the swirl. So you try again...again... again...

Now! The rod is a thing alive. The debris on the far shore seems to be drawing your line like a magnet. Now you're snagged! No, it's coming back out! Be careful...careful...

Pulse pounding, you hold the dripping net aloft, convinced anew that an 11-inch beaver pond brookie is the equal of any fish that swims.

The weight of the trout feels good in the old wicker creel as you begin casting again. Over there now. Never mind the deer fly just above your ear.

Would anyone else be crazy enough to call this fun?

You know the answer to that. Trout fishing addicts lurk everywhere, in all kinds of disguises. You'd never suspect the sanity of some of them.

So, you're not going to tell anyone where this place is. Nobody at all.

(07/24/75)

A BOONDOCKS REPORT

There are big doings in the boondocks these days.

A family of skunks has been turning our lawn into a ragged, brown rug. However, the grubs they seek were killing the grass anyway.

And there are other dramas unfolding, seldom seen. Such as:

A monarch butterfly fluttered by, bound for the milkweeds flowering in our fields. I followed with a camera. The butterfly was shy, so I crouched in ambush, waiting for it to pose within range of my lens.

I watched a bee buzzing among the blossoms. Suddenly it stopped, seeming to dangle from a flower with its wings stilled. I crept closer. A waxy white spider with slim purple stripes was retreating into the flower head. It seemed to disappear. However, its fangs still gripped the boldly-marked bee, now dead or paralyzed.

The spider's camouflage was almost incredible. But what happens when the milkweed blooms are gone? Is there another flower so suited to that spider's deadly game of hide and seek? Might the spider change appearance like a chameleon? Or will it die, leaving eggs dormant in a silken vault until spiderlings can find purple milkweeds in flower again?

For each answer the inquiring mind finds in nature, there are still more questions.

Our wild crops are maturing on schedule. The raspberry harvest is almost over, but the dogwoods now are laden with waxen fruit. Swelling grape clusters weigh heavily on the vines while elderberries are already being picked, still green. Prime suspects are the catbirds, mewing impatiently in the woods.

A redheaded woodpecker makes frequent sorties from the oak woods these days, its flight erratic, undulating, unlike the doves which dart like arrows from the pine grove each morning.

And often on sultry afternoons, a breeze will stir the lake, breathing sparkling life into the water; caressing sweaty brows.

All of those are small things, I'm sure, in the great scheme of things. Yet each is an event of some moment in the boondocks these summery days.

(07/24/71)

REQUIEM

A bluebird is singing; robins are chirping. Yet, the path seems lifeless, almost airless, as I walk the woods alone. Dash is dead. He was my pal; my partner. He was our dog.

A chipmunk scurries down the bank at my approach; pauses on a tree limb, seeming surprised that there has been no pursuit. Life may seem more serene for the chipmunks for a time, but the lithe hound they scolded was really their friend. He never caught a chipmunk, and those predators which could, such as roving cats and foxes, found Dash's domain dangerous hunting grounds.

He was an underprivileged puppy just six years ago. Born in a barn, ill-fed, full of fleas. His parentage was an uncertain combination of coonhound and cowdog, but he had his own pedigree. There was something appealing, promising, about his spirit.

At maturity he had a measure of dignity and devotion which made him an easy dog to live with. It would embarrass him to be treated like a lap dog, but he was always appreciative of a kind word or hand. He liked people; loved children.

As a hunter, his untiring persistence and able nose won admiration from any who followed him afield, including some who had scorned his humble origin.

Dash had apparently been ill for a long time, but his game heart masked most of the symptoms until he grew gaunt and weak. He developed a chronic, racking cough. Routine examinations and treatments availed nothing. Finally, a series of more elaborate tests revealed that he was diabetic and suffering from incurable anemia.

The report left me without hope. It seemed selfish, unkind, to put him through anything more. Feeling like a Judas, I signed his death warrant.

"It's a lot of money to pay for a dead dog," the veterinarian said sympathetically as he added up the bill. Then Dash was put quietly to sleep and I carried him to the car, tears streaming down my cheeks.

I buried him in a quiet corner of our woods in the shade of a big bur oak. It was a place he liked; a spot where there always seemed to be the scent of rabbit, squirrel or chipmunk to start his tail wagging.

The shiny green hulls of hickory nuts are swelling, beginning to bend the branches with their weight. Squirrels will soon discover that they can steal all of the nuts without reproach. Woodchucks will start excavating the hill again. Mice will sleep in the straw of the doghouse. Turtles will dig nests in the gravel driveway and gophers will burrow in the lawn. A man needs help to keep things in place around a country home.

Somewhere a puppy will be waiting to fill the vacuum, but I am not ready.

Mourning doves are sounding their melancholy notes from the old bur oak. My eyes are stinging, my throat is dry. The path seems to lead nowhere. Nowhere at all.

(07/25/69)

AUTUMN SIGNS

Summer is heading over the hill, with lengthening strides toward autumn. You can feel it in the coolness of morning dew before the sun sizzles it away. You can hear it in the conversations of young crows and scent it in the thistle patches.

Out our way, the evidence appears everywhere these days.

• A lanky doe with triplets in tow; the fawns already so tall that spots look out of place on their russet coats.

• Young raccoons hurrying awkwardly across a road as the sun is setting. Following mother to somebody's sweet corn patch, no doubt,

• Raspberries ripe, gayfeather blooming, lavender loosestrife petals drifting down the creek.

Cobweb across the entrance of an empty bluebird house, a woodcock's wing feather molted on the marsh trail, speckle-bellied young robins learning to out-hop bugs in the garden.

Although those are sufficient signs that summer is slipping away, the clincher has arrived in the mail. It is the perennial fall catalog from L.L. Bean, the old Maine mail order house, purveyor of such things as briarproof pants with suspender buttons which stay on, rubber-bottomed shoe pacs, floppy felt hats and similar necessities of life.

Except (alas) for the prices, many of those items have remained essentially unchanged during the decades I have been on Bean's mailing list. Why, just turning the pages is tantamount to taking the old boots and mackinaw, filled with memories, from the closet once more.

But I didn't open this one right away, The cover held me. There is a picture of a ruffed grouse, alertly looking off into a woods that gleams with autumn's gold.

I think I know what that bird has heard. It is the distant tinkle of a bell on a dog's collar.

Ah, there he is, a springer spaniel bounding through the leaves, stub tail vibrating. Did you ever see such a grin on a dog's face? My pulse quickens. My boots are weightless now. The little 20 gauge is poised....

Okay, turn the page. But it won't be long. Autumn is on the way.

(07/29/80)

SIGNALS

Mother bluebird perched on a fencepost, head cocked, watching her awkward young flutter after bugs.

Buck deer, body slender in sparse summer coat, antlers thick with velvet.

Lilies flaming like torches along a trail. Wild mints underfoot. Blueflags crowding up to a creek bank as if to admire their reflections.

These are times of subtle signs; soft, slow changes in scents and scenes and sounds. But there are surprises too. Such as that buck bounding out of a neighbor's tasseled cornfield, wearing a 10-point rack, already fully formed.

Realization dawns: Summer's moving on.

It has been the kind of summer idealized in songs and seed catalogs. The crops look fine. Acorns and nuts are going to be plentiful. Wild berries abound. Birds are reveling in the dogwoods, where red osiers bear pearly fruit.

Catbirds, cardinals, redwings, thrashers, orioles, vireos, grosbeaks, robins and chickadees. Those are among the regular residents. Lately there have been some newcomers too.

Barn swallows now appear daily, spending hours performing like stunt fliers above our driveway. Bugs must be easier to nab as they fly over the blacktop.

And bluebirds are back. They passed us by in spring because tree swallows occupied every house -- including several hastily built when the shortage was apparent. However, an occasional call or glimpse assured me that they had not gone far. Now they bring their latest brood to our garden, to teach them about tricky insects.

It is the time for lessons. A young raccoon finds that if you grab a crawdad wrong, it will grab you back. And the young crow learns that the world is a place where one might be pursued and pecked, just because of the way you look.

Summer has some stings for all of us. Green-eyed flies, whining mosquitos, pesky ticks and gnats. And raging storms that shake the earth, rend the sky; drive rivers from their banks. Oldtime summers like this are prone to such tantrums.

But they are soon forgiven. Look:

Rubies glowing in the honeysuckles. Nights sparkling with stars and fireflies. Mornings when mullein leaves are silvery with dew.

Catch such moments now, for we cannot hold them long.

Summer's moving on.

(07/31/78)

AUGUST

AUGUST AGAIN

The martins are forming long ranks on telephone lines, resting -- yet restless. One morning they will be gone.

The abrupt departure of martins always seems a surprise. One day it is summer. Lavender loosestrife borders the river and wasps are humming in the horsemints. The sound of cicadas saws the air.

Suddenly the martins vanish. We notice then that feathery white plumes are waving from the fireweed's seed pods; that fragile nightshade blossoms have become ruby berries; that the Solomon's seal fruits have turned dusky blue. All signs that summer is sidling away.

August is adolescence, but maturity must come soon, both for creatures which will leave us and those which will stay. Duck broods gain strength with longer flights each day. Dark splotches of color appear on the breast of the young pheasant rooster, and it starts to assert itself with raspy cackles. The young raccoon disdains a romp with its littermates to investigate ripening fruits. It soon will learn that tasseled corn swells its kernels with sweet milk.

August is harvest time. It is when impatient squirrels begin to take the still-green fruits from butternut, hazel and hickory. It is a time too, when many birds shed feathers frayed by summer's labors and don new traveling suits. The juvenile redheaded woodpecker will trade his gray cap for one of scarlet. Many other birds, however -- the tanagers, buntings and warblers -- change to more somber garb than they wear in spring. Almost unnoticed, they slip southward before the foliage falls.

There is yet much to be done. Autumn is still a lifetime away for the little yellow butterflies which flit along the shaded banks. Starry campions still shine there, and bergamots still raise their ragged heads near turks'-cap lilies in the lowland. Nearby, jewelweeds have just begun to bloom and asters have appeared. Wild cucumber vines, arrayed with feathery blossoms, writhe along the fencerows, wrestling weaker neighbors to the ground.

But August is here, and autumn is near, when martins perch in restless rows.

(08/08/64)

MUSKY ODDS

Hayward -- "I figure there's only 11 or 12 really good days a year for musky fishing," said Bob Becker, looking to the clouded sky for some encouragement.

"Let's see," I thought, *"The season is 208 days long. That makes the odds about 17 to one."*

"There's usually one week in August when the muskies hit for a while," Becker observed a bit later, while cranking a big, noisy surface plug back to the boat.

"Well, that's better," I mused. *"This week, the odds may be only four to one in favor of the fish."*

And the way musky fishermen figure, that's a good chance.

Such thinking would soon have any other kind of gambler garbed in a barrel. Not a musky angler. He'd take the barrel, fasten some hooks to it, and make a few more casts.

If there is anything certain about musky fishing, it is that the odds are always heavily in favor of the fish.

"Catch anything?" call the occupants of passing boats.

"No, we're musky fishing," you answer. And they nod in understanding.

You must know by now that the muskies have bested me again. I didn't catch a musky in two days of earnest endeavor. Bob Becker didn't catch any either. Nor did Rod Bahr or Bob Dreis or Jim Mense.

We did determine, however, that there is a large musky residing in

Teal Lake, just a few miles east of Hayward. Once it swirled behind a lure, leaving a curving wake which lapped against the shoreline. Another time, it stuck its tail out of the water THIS far! I judged that it was connected to a fish of 40 pounds or more.

We five had pitched camp on one of Teal Lake's state-owned islands. Bahr and Mense had come from Menomonie; Becker and Dreis from Spooner, to join me in an assault on yet another musky stronghold.

Musky anglers tend to gather in groups. They even organize into clubs which mount massive campaigns against the quarry. There are several explanations for that. It is well to have others to shout encouragement and advice, handle the net and take pictures in the unlikely event that a musky actually grabs your lure. It is also useful to have witnesses to back you up when you tell of the "follows" you have had.

(A "follow" is a musky trailing the lure, only to turn away without striking. Muskies do that a lot. Sometimes the same huge shadow will follow the lure again and again. Something like 100 "follows" equals one musky caught -- or a nervous breakdown, whichever comes first).

Mostly though, I think that musky anglers band together because misery loves company. Only another so afflicted can really understand the tortures of musky fever.

So we gathered around the campfire each night, applying brandy to our wounds and commiserating with each other about aching casting arms, the uncertainties of life and the exorbitant cost of musky baits.

Of course, I cannot tell you just where to find the hangout of that big fish. However, I'll give you a few clues:

We tried Rock Bar, Center Bar, Snag Bar, and every bay and weedbed on Teal Lake. Then we traveled through the thoroughfare to neighboring Lost Land Lake and fished around Duncan Point and Beaver Creek and

Tiddlewink Bar and the mouth of Wilson Creek. Somewhere around one of those places you might see a giant swirl or shadow. If you're lucky, you might even have a follow.

But then, there are other reasons for musky fishing. Like seeing a mother merganser skim across the water with her brood in tow. Like listening to loons at sunset. Like watching otters pop to the surface like jack-in-the-boxes, hissing their sentiments at our intrusion.

We will remember too, how the water lilies and spatterdock and pickerel weeds were in bloom, how the campfire was reflected in waves lapping the shore, and how, one night, the sky glowed with a dazzling display of northern lights. That was another reminder that summer was waning fast.

We broke camp reluctantly, all the while making plans for the next time. The only way to beat the odds in musky fishing is to keep trying... keep trying...keep trying.

"And we do," I was thinking during the long drive home. *"Maybe that is the oddest thing of all."*

(08/08/77)

THE WHISTLE

The other day I discovered that my whistle was gone. I hadn't used it for a long time, but its loss was troubling. Long ago I strove mightily to own such a whistle, and when it finally came to me, at age 10, it was with a lifetime guarantee:

"You godt idt now foreffer," I was assured by Old Hans.

His Teutonic accent, a haystack beard and a great cud of chewing tobacco blurred his pronouncement, but the promise was clear. No matter how fervently my elders might pray for it, I would never misplace that whistle.

So imagine my disappointment when, after only six decades, it was gone.

The loss was discovered during a hike along the river. My dog was lingering far behind, reluctant to leave a tree which sheltered a sassy squirrel. I had forgotten the whistle I usually wear around my neck on such hikes. But no matter. I had another right at my fingertips.

Maybe you know the kind. You just tuck a couple of fingers into your mouth, curl your tongue just so, and *PUFF!* Properly done, it produces a painfully sharp blast. Because it was really much too loud for comfort, I had rarely called upon the talent in recent years, but it would be just the thing to bring that dawdling dog to attention.

I raised my fingers to my lips and blew. Only a hiss emerged. I tried repeatedly with similar results until Brighton, tiring of the squirrel's impudence, finally bounded back, cocking her head quizzically at my continued huffing.

My thoughts were swirling slowly, like the eddies in the river. Memories bobbed to the surface like bits of flotsam. I was remembering how well the whistle had served me during boyhood. A kid who could whistle like *that* got a certain amount of respect from his peers.

I pretty much abandoned using that whistle after joining the Navy. There my shipboard duties included trilling on a bosun's pipe, another whistle with much authority. Its shrill notes roused sleepy sailors from their bunks, told them when to scrub the decks, and reminded them of sundry other shipboard routines.

I was weary of loud whistles after that. While training a succession of hunting dogs, I even bought a whistle which was nearly inaudible to human ears. Still, I always knew that my gift from Old Hans was there if I needed it.

Old Hans lived in a ramshackle little house about a mile down a dusty road from my grandparents' farm. He didn't own much land, but had a garden for himself and some pasture for his goats. His herd consisted of a few nannies and one belligerent billy with a serious case of body odor.

"Hard to tell who smells worse, Old Hans or that billy goat," Grandma sometimes observed.

But pungent as he might be, Old Hans was a valued neighbor. He unfailingly showed up at threshing time and he often helped on other occasions. Sounds of axe and crosscut saw usually summoned him to Grandpa's woodlot, which wasn't far from his shack. Then, with hardly more than a nod, he would pitch in with zest and skill, helping build new walls of firewood against the advance of another winter.

"Nobody can keep up with that old geezer when he's on the other end of a crosscut saw, and I'll bet he could skin a muskrat with his axe,"

Grandpa said admiringly.

Old Hans wielded the tool of a real woodsman -- a double-bitted axe with one edge beveled for heavy chopping; the other honed keen as a knife for slicing small limbs. Both edges were kept sharp and bright on his grindstone.

He could sharpen anything on that marvelous machine. Neighbors brought axes and adzes, sickles and scissors. Perched on the rig's iron seat, Old Hans would pump the foot pedal until the stone hummed a low monotone. Then, deftly gauging the angle by eye and by feel, he would touch the edge to the whirling wheel. Sparks showered like Independence Day fireworks as the stone shrilled against the steel.

I often watched, entranced. Sparks leaped at the old man's weathered hands and danced from his wire-rimmed glasses, but he never flinched. With the intentness of a symphony conductor, he was listening for the proper pitch:

"It must sing; never cry or scream," he told me.

Cradled over the wheel was a tin pitcher. It was tilted frequently to sprinkle water on the stone, flushing away residues and cooling the work. Too much heat would spoil the temper, Old Hans explained. And only rain water would do, he declared.

Knives got special treatment from an assortment of oilstones. Old Hans would stroke a blade on first one; then another and another, until a touch against a thumbnail told him that the edge was ready for "stropping" on a wide leather strap.

"You could shave with a cleaver after Old Hans got through with it," Grandpa marveled.

"Too bad he don't sharpen one for himself then, and hack off that rat's nest of a beard," Grandma said.

"Nonetheless, Old Hans was always invited to her table after a days work with her men, and she remarked that he was always an appreciative and mannerly guest.

Money was scarce in those days, but it appeared that Old Hans had pretty much learned to do without it. If you needed anything fixed, be it a harness or a door hinge, he could probably do it, and he bartered his labor and talents for nearly everything he needed or craved: A sack of grain, a pair of home-knit socks, an old horse blanket, or a home-cooked meal were all taken as fair exchange.

One year, striving to earn some hard cash, Grandpa planted a patch of tobacco. Maybe the soil was wrong. The tobacco ended up as clusters of evil-smelling, tar-colored leaves hanging in the granary.

"Maybe they'll keep the mice and rats out of the grain bins," Grandma observed wryly.

However, late that fall. Old Hans volunteered to take that tobacco as recompense for his work in the woods. For many months thereafter, his spittle was black and the smoke from his pipe could fumigate a barn. Still, he seemed more than pleased with the deal. He even asked Grandpa if he planned to grow some more. He did not.

For me, having Old Hans as a neighbor was better than having Santa living just down the road. When an uncle gave me an old .22 rifle, Old Hans repaired the sights and replaced the broken stock with one crafted from walnut. Another time, surprised to learn that I had no skis, he selected two white ash planks from the treasures in his shed loft and set to work. During the next several days, using only a few ancient-looking hand tools, he sawed and planed, smoothed and grooved, steamed and bent, curved and cambered, until those rough boards were transformed into wings for my feet.

Well, at least they were *supposed* to be wings. Broad and sturdy, with three bottom grooves, they were intended to be "chumping" skis. A few spectacular spills soon convinced me that I had no future as a ski jumper, but those skis served me in lieu of snow shoes for many years.

(Much later, after cross-country skiing became popular in this country, I tried a pair of real cross-country skis and promptly fell down. Compared to my old reliables, the darned things were just too skinny and skittish).

Grandpa said that Old Hans was Austrian. He had lived alone a long time and nobody seemed to know much about him. And he shrugged when asked his age, About 80, most believed.

He sometimes sounded gruff, but I remember his kindness and patience. He taught me how to sharpen a knife; then use it to make a flute from a slippery elm stick.

And yes, I well remembered during that reverie along the river, how he had shown me how to whistle.

Oh, I could tweet through my teeth all right, but Old Hans could really *WHISTLE!* When he poked his fingers into his mouth and blew, things happened. Cows swallowed their cuds and hounds started howling two miles away. It was a talent I much admired.

I gagged myself a thousand times that summer I was 10. I just couldn't find the right way to arrange my fingers and tongue. Old Hans assured me that I had a whistle in there somewhere. When I neared despair, he counseled me to keep trying. He explained that everyone is made a little differently, so each has to find their own whistle.

Then came that late summer day when cicadas were singing in the trees. Grandma called them "seven year locusts" and said I should beware of their sting, so I was avoiding the trees. I was sprawled in the shade of the corn crib, still huffing away, when a wispy little note slipped past my fingers. My heart raced! Panting and puffing, I made tiny adjustments and kept trying. And finally, there it was!

A piercing blast rattled the corrugated roof of the woodshed and Grandma's pullets were scattering in panic.

"What in tarnation...!" Grandma shouted. But I was already galloping across the back pasture, taking the shortcut to Old Hans' place. He was in his shed, milking a goat.

"Mister Hans!," I croaked, breathless, unable to say more.

"Ja, I *heard*," he answered, a smile parting his beard.

A nudge of my dog's nose brought me back from my reverie. That had all been a long time ago. Grandma, Grandpa, Old Hans, all long gone. And now the whistle was gone too. I felt the weight of the years.

Yesterday I took another stroll along the river. It was one of those dozy summer afternoons when cicadas are singing to the sun. I paused in the shade of a big cottonwood while the dog wallowed in the river. A couple of young anglers were sitting on the far bank. Otherwise, I had the scene to myself.

Somewhere above my head a cicada sounded its siren, awakening more memories. I remembered Old Hans confiding that the sound wasn't made by insects at all, but by elves at their grindstones, "scharpening sickles" for the harvest.

Idly, I joined the tips of my left forefinger and thumb, raised them to my mouth and huffed. An explosion could not have been more startling. My whistle was back, and Old Hans himself had never done better! The cicadas had stopped shrieking. The frightened dog was splashing ashore.

The boys on the far bank had leaped to their feet. I waved. Then, with exaggerated motions, I poked my fingers into my mouth and whistled once more. That was enough. It hurt my ears.

As I started back down the trail, Brighton walked at heel, her ears and tail drooping. She was wondering what she had done to warrant such a sharp summons. I stopped to scratch her ears.

The cicada concert was resuming. I hummed a happy accompaniment, smiling as I thought about those boys across the river.

I guessed that they would be huffing and puffing and gagging all the way home.

(08/15/97)

HARVEST TIME

Deep green seas of tasseled corn; golden isles of grain. Dawns shining in dew; days shimmering in haze. Harvest time. And if you'll look in God's gardens, beyond the farthest furrow, you'll find many gleaners gathering for the feast.

Impatient catbirds are picking still-ripening elderberries. Young robins, breasts still speckled, are perching in the dogwoods. Wild grapes are maturing fast, and, though a late frost nipped the vines, there'll be bunches enough for the early birds. And for the raccoons' dessert after they've wiped the corn milk from their faces.

Soon too, there'll be the thin, sweet notes of waxwings in the cedars, and the chuckle of squirrels filling their bins with another bounty of hickory nuts. Already the hickory hulls are tinged with tan, bulging as if to burst their seams. Already the burr oak acorns are peeking from under their fringed caps. A squirrel scolds when we bend a bough to see. Isn't the crop rightly his? Didn't his forbears plant the seed?

The chatter brings a kingbird, sweeping boldly. His mate watches calmly from a nearby nest, confident that he can cope with this intruder Soundless, he alights on a limb at eye level, poised, fanning his white-banded tail in warning. There is neither bluff nor boast in his manner as he watches us depart.

Although insects are the usual fare for his family, the ripening fruits do not escape the notice of the kingbird. Later, he will feast on dogwood berries or nip a few elderberries, and no bird will bar his way to the bushes.

Except, perhaps, a hummingbird which often visits the swamp. Swift and rapier-beaked, he seems to dart at bigger birds for sheer mischief. None of them are competitors for stores of nectar, but he seems to revel in showing off his aerobatics and armament.

Nature's crops come in wondrously varied shapes and sizes. Most are seeds, stored by small mammals or relished by resident and migrant birds. The chipmunk gathers seed pods from the wild geraniums. The ruffed grouse seeks the seeds of touch-me-nots. Even such banes of man as crabgrass, burdock, ragweed and goldenrod set banquets for many birds.

The ruby glow of nightshade berries in every marshy place is evidence of their place on the menu. Birds distribute seeds of many favorite foods in their droppings. It is one of nature's clever strategies.

Not all the harvest is taken at once. The rusty spires of sumac and shiny red hips of wild rose are often ignored while more succulent fare is to be had. Yet, in winter, or the bleakness of early spring, they may mean life to a hungry bird.

Wildlife has a genetic memory of lean times. Even young squirrels, although they have never seen a winter, work diligently to hide a winter's supply of acorns. The nuthatch does the same, tucking its treasures under the shaggy bark or the hickories. The deer's share of the same bounty is stored as hard, white tallow, fuel for those frigid times ahead.

In recent weeks the woods have been relatively quiet, dozing in the sun. But now the busy time begins. Where nature sows, even as where man tills, there is a harvest to be reaped.

(08/16/65)

SUMMER WAS

Sometime there was summer. Enough, it seems, to persuade the northern hardwoods that there has been a season's quota.

Fiery flashes of color already brighten the woods these days. all the more surprising and beautiful because of the lush greenery surrounding.

Some sumacs are aglow. Bunchberries have turned crimson. The last of the raspberries are dead ripe. Brackens are browning along the trails.

So, sometime, summer was.

Young grouse are skulking under alder and aspen, fluttering away at the hen's beckoning. Duck broods are circling their home ponds, strengthening wings for the long fall flights. Adolescent pheasants are uttering sounds which now resemble real crowing and cackling.

Already the jewelweed and wild cucumber are in bloom. How soon blackbirds have begun swarming into the cattails at dusk. How quickly mewing catbirds have arrived to harvest purpling elderberries. All those are sudden signs that summer has been.

There are summers that just turtle along from spring to fall. This one has scampered like a chipmunk, to and fro, full speed and stop. More than the maples have been confused. Some spruces and pines have droopy looks because sharp frosts bit at this year's growth. Severe frosts were noted in the north during May, June and July.

The wild cherry crop -- a favorite food of birds and bears in August -- has been nearly a total loss. Raspberries and blackberries fared somewhat better, but the blueberries were hard hit, first by frost and then by a dry spell.

The oaks will make up for many such deficiencies. Somehow most of them escaped serious frost damage. Acorns, a staple for many species of wildlife, will soon be falling in profusion. Bears, squirrels, grouse, and even ducks will feast on that bounty this fall. And deer will paw for them far into the winter.

Swallows are forming military ranks on wires. Songbirds are conducting singing lessons for their now self-sufficient young.

Where trilliums bloomed in spring, the moist woods now are decorated with arrays of mushrooms, some yellow, some red, shaggy and smooth, tiny or tall. And along the woods edges the lilies have faded; the blue asters bloom.

So it seems that summer was, sometime.

(08/17/72)

SLIPPING AWAY

Eagle River -- It all looks familiar. Wisps of early morning fog ghosting down the river. Dew sparkling in the jewelweeds. Roadsides aglow with goldenrod. Purple asters suddenly everywhere. And yes, even flickers of flame in the hardwoods.

Autumn? In August? Not quite, but there are abundant signs that summer's on the run.

Deer, still in russet summer coats, are as bright as new pennies against the shaded forest. But look again. The spots are fading on dappled fawns and kingly bucks are wearing crowns again. Their antlers, still sheathed in velvet, will soon be bared and honed to impress both doe and foe.

There is a shivery anticipation in these mint-fresh mornings. And there is consolation for those who feel that Wisconsin winters come too soon and stay too long. The calendar decrees that there will be yet a month of summer -- and summer always saves the best until last.

Now there are days aflutter with butterflies, azure skies adrift with cottony clouds, fallow fields laced with cobwebs; woodlands swelling again with birdsong.

You can hear the young voices -- the buzzy calls of adolescent crows; tentative notes from recently fledged thrushes and orioles. Adult birds, meantime, sound off with almost springlike vigor. Might they be giving their youngsters singing lessons?

Science says that they are simply responding to signals from the sun. Certain hormones stir in birds, both spring and fall, as the sun nears the equinox. So the cardinal whistles, the pheasant crows; the grouse beats its drum as summer marches off. The fledglings listen and learn.

Songs are not the only things young birds study as summer wanes. Recruit redwings rehearse that uncanny aerial choreography that enables each member of a flock to twist and turn in unison. Young teal test pinions with leaping takeoffs and splashy landings. Families of swallows swoop across ponds, glancing from the surface like skipping stones as they dip to drink.

The swallows will go first, and soon. And then the teal. From nesting sites to staging areas, their fall migration has already begun.

Such signs do not go unnoticed in these latitudes. Woodpiles grow. Woolen mackinaws are being aired. Hunting prospects begin to rival fishing and the weather as a favorite topic in small town cafes.

Don't count summer out. Lavender plumes of fireweed and burnt-orange blossoms of hawkweed still compete with the goldenrods. The sun still makes short work of chilly mornings and dragonflies still rustle through golden afternoons.

But the signs are clear. Blackberries are ripening. Acorns are falling. Ripened rose hips gleam like tiny red apples. Burdocks are sharpening their bristles, preparing to grab rides on bushy tails.

At each turn of the trail, the path looks more familiar. We have been this way before.

Not far ahead now, is where we bid summer farewell.

(8/20/85)

THE COUNTDOWN

There are mornings now when luminous mists wreath the land...when filmy tents spun by caterpillars shroud branches with silver veils...when a cuckoo's metered calls sound like a metronome, like the pendulum of a clock.

The countdown has begun. Ducks circle on whispering wings. Blackbirds swarm across the sky. Rows of swallows watch from wires. The time for long fall flights is near.

Catbirds are exulting in elderberries. Cardinals and orioles are picking the last of the wild cherries. Squirrels are snipping walnuts, still sheathed in sticky green hulls. Bur oak acorns are shedding their fringed caps. Hickory nuts will soon be thumping to the ground.

Happy days these, for squirrels and birds.

Summer still grasps at straws. There are times, bright and breathless, when cicadas shriek and the land parches as in an oven.

But autumn's approach is advertised in cackles of adolescent pheasants and in feathery white blooms of wild cucumber draping marshland borders. It is seen in shining boneset blossoms, in bright patches of sunflowers; in vervain, thistle and jewelweed...

Green barbs stiffen on sticktights. Thornapples wink like tiny red lights on the hillside. Bittersweet berries gleam. Butterflies flicker like flames through the shadowed woods.

There are dusks now when nighthawks swoop in squadrons where before they flew in pairs. The wood peewee whistles its constant question; then plaintively answers itself. Then there is a coolness, and a quiet, until the night sounds begin.

In the dark there is a rustling of 'possums in the cherry trees, soft hooting of owls, the strumming of a bullfrog; the occasional crash of an aspen felled by the beavers.

Sometimes too, there are the bird-like conversations of raccoons. Those which were born in a hollow oak behind our house are a third grown now. Still ungainly, they seem to be going downhill, even as they amble across level ground. In search of provender or adventure, they romp in newfound freedom from parenting.

It seems but yesterday that I watched the last of the litter leave the den, masked eyes wide with awe as its mother descended headfirst, the little one held gently in her jaws. Now they gorge on grapes so sour they would screw your eyes shut. But they know where to find an antidote of wild plums, plump and sweet.

But what I began to tell you is that there now are mornings glittering with diamonds of dew. And that the chipmunks, looking fat and sleepy, are emerging later each day. There's a cidery smell in the breeze where apples have fallen from forgotten trees, and wine tints are appearing in sumac, ivy and dogwood.

The time of fruit and ferment is here. And who is immune to its intoxication?

Not I.

(08/21/68)

DEWDROPS

Shall we talk about dew? Would you walk wet footed around a little marsh this dawn, watching diamonds drip from foliage, seeing strings of crystal beads sparkle on old fence wires?

Then come...

Those little orange lanterns winking in the early light? Jewelweeds, leaves spattered with silver. Did you know that the leaves, held underwater, appear altogether silvery? Children know such alchemy but adults frequently forget.

Those feathery white plumes? Wild cucumber. Come closer:

See how the vine's tendrils coil tightly, deftly clutching what they touch. This tendril has captured a dewdrop. Peer through the encircled droplet and see, much magnified, the intricate detail in the blossom behind it.

A dewdrop, you see, brings beauty in many ways.

Consider the Indian cups, those tall, yellow flowers just down the trail. Their leaves join at the plants' sturdy, square stems, forming cups which hold clear pools of dew. Each now mirrors the marsh; the sky.

On the nightshade's lobed leaves, droplets cling in perfect hemispheres until the sun appears. Then they droop into tear-shaped prisms, exploding the first rays of day, showering the scene with bits of rainbow.

But time is fleeting. Look quickly:

Spiderweb...fine filigree of platinum, set with gems. Thistle...deep purple brushed with silver. Ironweed...lavender with a neon glow.

62

Foxglove...yellow beakers aglow. Mullein...velvet leaves whitened as if by frost. Mushrooms...caps shining like gilded domes.

And then the spell is broken. A jay scolds, a catbird complains, a woodpecker wickers. A mosquito, buzzing feebly, alights on a sunlit limb to warm its numb body.

Brightening sunbeams search the earth. Dewdrops blaze brief defiance at their discovery; then disappear into wisps of mist drifting through the cattails.

Another late summer day has begun. Fresh and clean. Bathed with dew.

(08/25/65)

NEW WINGS

Chirping crickets. Singing cicadas. Swallows forming ranks on roadside wires. Green burs clinging to a spaniel's ears.

August on the run.

Catbirds celebrating a bounty of wild cherries. Raccoons reveling in ripening corn. Purple loosestrife parading along the creek banks, marching to a tune hummed by bees.

Now summer's sleepy pace quickens; the sun lengthens its strides across the sky.

Swelling acorns peeking from under their caps. Wild geese calling. Frayed feathers found in the garden -- cast-offs from a blackbird's wing, a robin's tail, a cardinal's breast.

August is a month of hurried miracles; of young wings strengthened, old ones renewed. Consider the marvels in the way birds molt:

Because feathers wear out, all birds undergo changes of plumage at least twice a year. Some species do it oftener.

For swallows (and other species that can't afford to be grounded) the molt is not only gradual but symmetrical. The bird is never hindered by simultaneous loss of too many flight feathers, or by losing more on one side than another. From the time it leaves the nest, a swallow must fly to live. So these days, the fledglings of July cannot be distinguished from their parents as they swoop after airborne insects.

For the geese now winging over the creek each morning, the molt was far different. The parents were flightless during much of the time the brood was growing up. But there is no great need for waterfowl to fly during that time. There is ample food to be found in the water and along the banks -- and there are those flightless young to keep constant watch over.

Another small wonder is the "eclipse" plumage which drake ducks don during the flightless period. You can easily observe it in the mallards on park ponds. Those gaudy greenheads haven't gone away. They just look a lot like hens.

Those drab eclipse feathers provide far better camouflage than the drake's dress suit -- and there is an obvious advantage in being less conspicuous when you can't fly from danger.

Geese, being bigger and having less need to hide from predators, dispense with the complication of changing color during their molt.

Now there are scarlet spatters in the sumacs and creeper vines. Now ruby berries glowing in the nightshade. Now yellow tints in aspen leaves.

Reminders that feathers shed in August will soon be hidden under autumn leaves.

(08/30/83)

SEPTEMBER

SO LONG SUMMER

A cobweb, silvery with dew, is woven across the doorway of a birdhouse this morning. A spider has seen the vacancy sign left by the last occupants, a brood of tree swallows.

So long, summer.

Now catbirds celebrate in the elderberries bordering the marsh. Jewelweed blossoms shine in the wetlands. Ground cherries nod like Japanese lanterns in fallow fields.

Hello September.

Now each day brings new reminders: Deer beginning to change to gray winter coats, although their antlers are still in velvet. Burs, still green, but sharp enough to bite my spaniel's ears. Cidery scents of windfallen apples in an old orchard. Redwings flocked. Crows convened.

On your mark, migrants.

Robins perched in wild cherry trees, surfeited by the bounties found there. The small, dark fruit is dead ripe, but still more stone than flesh; more sour than sweet. However, the bitterness is only in the beginning. The sweet, tart flavor lingers. If you think about it, a lot of life's like that.

Squirrels snipping unripe acorns; impatiently eyeing hickory limbs. Young ducks on training flights in brisk dawns. Trails bordered with aster, gayfeather, gentian and goldenrod. Geese pointed like arrows in the soft, blue sky.

This way autumn. But take your time.

(09/02/73)

WEB WONDERS

Now come mornings veiled in luminous mist; cobwebs silver with dew. Now the milkweed spews silken seeds and thistledown drifts across dazzling afternoons.

Wispy clues, those, that autumn is near. But evidence enough for spiders, who don't need calendars to tell them that summer is spinning away.

I don't know what it is that bestirs spiders so in autumn. We cross the fields, the dog and I, when day is still out of focus in the fog. And webs glisten everywhere. Draped in weeds, strung on fence wires; woven from leaf to limb of dogwoods. Acres of them. Thousands and tens of thousands. Each a geometric marvel, a world of wonder. All so heavily jeweled with dew that they literally explode, vaporize, at the merest touch.

Things I do know of spiders make them no less a mystery. A tiny spider can spin a filament so long and fine that it clings to the air. Like a balloon, it carries its rider aloft and away. To where? And why?

Spiders have been studied enviously by makers of fishing lines, for the finest nylon monofilament are poor imitations of a spider's strands. In fact, no fiber spun in man's laboratories can approach the strength of the spider's silk. To give you an idea, a strand one inch in diameter would hold more than 74 tons without breaking. That is three times stronger than a steel cable that size.

And did you know that the spider manufactures more than one kind of silk? For the strong strands supporting the web, there is one formula;

for the sticky, elastic, crossing strands there is another.

But, getting back to seasonal things, if you don't believe in the prognostications of spiders, there are other signs:

Lavender petals of loosetrife have joined the first fallen aspen leaves in the currents of the creeks. The marsh edge is aglow with lanterns of jewelweed and plumed with airy blooms of wild cucumber.

Now is the time of the goldenrod and blue aster, of fire flickering in the maple and catching in the tinder of the sumac. Now catbirds rejoice in elderberries and squirrels shuck hickory nuts from fat, green hulls. Now the nightshade's rubies are glowing and Solomon's seal berries are dusky blue.

There is a shimmering in the fields these misty mornings, as sunbeams touch the dew. It may be an illusion, a trick of light, but it looks like summer is struggling there. Caught in tiny silver bonds.

(09/08/77)

A COUNTRY CREEK

The day has been strident with the sound of the cicada. Bees buzz softly against drooping heads of sunflowers. (Researchers say a bee's hum drops from the middle key of A to E when it is tired. These sound like weary bees).

The afternoon heat has wilted even the wind, but now red-eyed and near-spent, the sun is settling to the horizon. A toad, dozing in a shaded corner of the garden, blinks into wakefulness. I have paused in the garden to pull some carrots, but now it is time to stroll down to the creek. The spaniel, quickly reading my intent, is panting his approval.

Across the field, past the old hickory and into the oak woods. Down a path bordered by shadbush and dogwood. Along a weathered plank walk through cattail and willow.

I pause along the way to marvel at a jade green chrysalis stitched with gold. It is a magic cradle, awaiting the awakening of a Monarch butterfly. And hazelnuts in fringed green coats. And feathery plumes of wild cucumber blooms. And creeper vines already aglow in autumn hues.

The dog sniffs where a woodcock probed for worms, where a rabbit slept, where a raccoon reached for ripened grapes. At the creek we stop, silent for uncounted minutes, watching underwater weeds undulate in the clear currents. Wisps of mist have begun to rise in the deepening shadows.

A deerfly, a stubborn survivor from the swarms of early August, weakly circles my head. A swat, and its crumpled form is floating in the creek amid fallen petals of loosestrife, a bit of bark, and dark flecks of other flotsam.

A fat, green sunfish sorts them out from its lookout in the weeds. I watch the fish drift into the current, like a reflection in imperfect glass. It poises for a moment; then swirls faster than the eye can follow. The fly is gone; the fish has returned to its lair.

The dog watches all this intently. You might think that he is only peering at his reflection, but that dog is a student of nature. I wish he could tell me all he knows.

Behind us on the hill, a bluebird family is flitting through the trees, discussing the day's doings. There was only one brood on our place this year, but survival was good. There are six.

A flock of ducks flies by, high in the waning light. The dog whimpers as though he too feels the pull of their wings.

Mosquitoes whine as we turn back up the path, but their bites are nothing. The abrasions of the day have been soothed. Men seek truth and solace in many places, in bottles and in books. They are found most easily, I think, along a country creek.

(09/03/75)

A TIME TO ENJOY

Whoa now, Autumn! The sun's been galloping across the sky as though winter were nipping at its heels. And I don't care what the weatherman said, that was frost slushing up my boots as I roamed through some lowlands this morning.

Autumn's the time the outdoorsman anticipates above all, and yet it takes us unaware, unprepared. And its stay, however long, is always far too brief for what there is to be done.

Never mind the storm windows or the fall plowing. I'm talking about important things like walking down sun-dappled woods trails, surrounded by the crisp scents and kaleidoscope scenes of an autumn morning.

I mean bidding goodbye to a stream wreathed with mist as the night chill descends and feeling the weight of a couple of good trout in the creel as you turn back toward the road.

I'm thinking of coonhounds singing to a frosty night and a hot scent, and of a cock grouse strutting a stump stage and drumming to the moon.

I'm anxious now to feel icy water clasp my waders while a fall-fat walleye strains my line and dusk deepens on my favorite river.

And where maples are reflected like a torchlight parade around the lake, a musky is waiting. I can almost hear its stomach growling.

That tremulous little tune in the autumn air? Woodcock rising from the alder bottoms. And that bugling, of coarse, is a goose in the marsh, beckoning new arrivals.

Whistling winds and wood ducks and widgeon. Hushed conversations of owls and resounding beaver splashes as night descends in the sloughs.

Pheasants rocketing away like feathered fireworks. Dogs with happy faces and burrs in their ears. Hickory nuts plopping and squirrels scampering, and deer battling saplings to hone antlers, shedding their velvet sheaths.

Salmon surging into rivers. Brown trout, rainbows, and even lake trout moving out of the deeps.

It all seems to happen at once, to end too soon. Maybe it's just as well. Maybe if there were more time to taste it all, every year, fall's flavor would lose its tang. Maybe the magic would be gone.

But those risks I'd be willing to run.

Easy now Autumn. Let's take the long way. We have a lot of stops to make before you go.

(09/11/75)

SUMMER GOODBYES

Well, there goes summer.

You can still see her waving from the fields, robed in gayfeather and goldenrod, Pale asters woven in her straw-colored hair. Those are traveling clothes. That's not a beckoning then. It's goodbye.

A fickle one she has been. Tardy, aloof, often cool. Yet, there is no denying that she was beautiful and dutiful. Her crops have flourished in garden, field and woods.

So now the oaks are bent with browning acorns, and mottled hulls hang heavy in the hickories, and the creek banks are jeweled with nightshade's rubies and dogwood's pearls.

We followed summer's trail in the dew at dawn, the dog and I.

Across a field where cobwebs were cast like fragile nets to catch the first sparks of day.

Where dragonflies, numbed by the night chill, clung to brittle stalks, their outstretched wings silvery as frost.

Where the monarch butterfly's chrysalis clung to a milkweed, a glistening green cradle stitched with gold.

Where young bluebirds chorused softly from a fence wire.

Summer has said her farewells in the marsh, where bidens beam and cattails sway and tamaracks brood. But her perfume lingers there. Catbirds, in varied voices, celebrate the bounty of elderberries she left behind.

An ancient oak groaned on a nearby hill, for this summer was surely its last.

Hollow as a drum, the old tree has been a valued occupant of our lands. It has been home for squirrel, flicker, wood duck, raccoon and owl. For many years it has seemed near death, but each spring its gnarled crown has turned bravely green again. However, now the massive trunk has split almost from crown to ground. When winter further brittles its old bones our old friend must fall. Then we will say our last goodbys at the fireplace, pushing winter away, remembering summers gone.

Another old oak was home to a colony of bees this summer. The bees are sleeping later these days, for they have labored long and well. Their honey is safe from us. The security we offer is small enough payment for tending countless blossoms since early spring.

So now burs are clinging to the spaniel's fur. Robins are flocked. Nighthawks are flying in squadrons. Blackbirds are storming across the sky.

Looking back, summer sees fall's approaching fires. She gathers the mists of a morning around her and swirls slowly down the trail.

Next week then, she will be gone.

(09/17/74)

MEETING FALL

Day was awakening, yawning, its breath softening silvery frost on browning brackens, stirring the stillness of sleepy aspens, slowly swirling through the bog mists.

Autumn's approach was announced in the sighs of dawn this day. Impatient, I have headed north to meet it. Come along:

Sumacs have been blushing all along the route -- through Antigo, Merrill, Rhinelander; Eagle River. Sparks are glimmering in the maples. Soon they will blaze into torches, marking the way for autumn's color guards and the parade to follow.

The ranks are assembling. Flocks of flickers flash golden wings along the winding backroads. There are squadrons of blackbirds. Ducks are practicing formations.

Yellow leaves are riding down the rivers. The riffles look inviting, and the flyrod still rides with me, but the trout season has ended on inland streams.

When I stopped in Merrill to see him, Trapper Morrison told of catching a limit of brookies that last evening of the season. He'd had them with fried green tomatoes for breakfast. Then, pitying the envy in my eyes, he promised that next year he'll show me where. But I must not tell.

Near Manitowish Waters a doe was leading a lanky fawn across the highway. The doe's coat was patchy -- summer's rust already giving way to winter's gray -- but the fawn still wore spots.

Manitowish Waters. The name has music in it. There is romance in many of the Indian names. And there is color and beauty in those bequeathed by the French: Bois Brule, Eau Claire, Lac du Flambeau.

However, there is also poetry to be found in some places named in our own tongue: Sparkling Lake. Diamond Lake. How aptly they glittered at the glance of the sun.

Blue asters are blooming bravely along the way to the Turtle-Flambeau Flowage. The road was shimmering, still wet from recent rain. It has been a wet, lush summer in the north. The berries and chokecherries are many, and the bears are fat.

At Scully's Sports Shop in Park Falls they were talking about hunters with truckloads of dogs who come from as far as the Carolinas to hunt bears each September. Yet, there seem to be as many bears as ever, it was agreed.

A raven flapped away as I rounded a curve. The sun struck its ebony wings as it banked at treetop level. For that moment, the bird looked as sleek as polished granite. An illusion.

Ravens are really raffish looking birds, heavy of beak, with tousled throat feathers and a rascally glint of eye. However, I hesitate to pass judgment on them, for I suspect that they know more about me than I do of them.

I do know that there is wild beauty in the raven's varied calls. Especially on those still winter days when the raven is alone in the icy sky.

Such days seem near again. Even in late afternoon, in the deep shade, the chill lingers. On the way to Butternut, I stopped to see Ed Robinson. I wanted to ask how the walleyes were biting. But Ed wasn't home. Guiding a float trip down the Flambeau River probably. Or maybe trying for sturgeon if he hasn't got a customer this fine day.

Connie Waterman, my old friend at the Prentice ranger station, warned that construction work made Highway 13 rough going for many miles. It was a good excuse to meander westward. down some well-remembered back roads, and inspect the grouse cover here and there.

It felt good to stretch, to poke along in the aspens and alders, thrilling again to the flush of a grouse and twittering rise of a woodcock. Soon I will return to seek them in earnest.

I followed the Black River, south from Hatfield, until the canoe landing at the mouth of Hall's Creek beckoned me to stop again. Jays cussed my intrusion and a squirrel joined in, sassy, scolding. There the river's clear currents broke white over rocks and curved into dark eddies, casting their own spell.

Night fell. The air had become cold; dense. I cranked the windows shut as I headed south again. The scent of sweet ferns, crushed by my boots, was heavy in my nostrils. In the beam of the headlights, the sumacs glowed like embers. An autumn wind will soon fan them into flame.

(09/20/71)

A CLASS ACT

Autumn arrived today with a dash of color and a touch of class.

Softening frost laid a silver carpet across the low meadow where I met this autumn's dawn. Brave blue bottle gentians gleamed like lights to mark the path.

Asters, palest blue and deepest purple, mingled in crowds of goldenrod and bur marigold.

Summer' passing was marked by faded gayfeather and bursting milkweed pods and the lingering scent of mint. Autumn was heralded by geese calling from a horizon tufted with hurrying clouds.

I followed to the woods edge, where flocks of robins and flutterings of warblers danced on dogwood branches, where nightshade berries hung were draped like ruby necklaces; where dusky hemispheres of fruit hung from carrion flower vines.

Yellow, mottled leaves waved from the hickories, where a bounty of nuts are attended by a celebration of squirrels. Along a little country road there was a redundance of wild grapes, and winey hues drenched the sumacs and cherry trees. Here and there, autumn's torch had already touched the maples and left a glow in the red oaks.

Apples and bittersweets ornamented the gnarled remnants of a long-abandoned farm orchard. A row of pumpkins, big and golden as rising harvest moons, beamed from a roadside stand.

Bluebirds, always loathe to leave come autumn, lingered in the sun, singing of a summer come and gone.

And then, when the last of the morning mists were gone, the air was crisp and clear. From Lapham Peak, south of Delafield, one could see the cathedral spires of Holy Hill etched against the northern sky, some 15 miles away.

Autumn, that was a dazzling premiere performance. This reviewer wishes you a long run with many curtain calls.

Encore! Well done. Encore!

(09/22/75)

AN UNPLANNED
PLEASURE

Dawn arrived in swirls of fog, veiling a promise of a dazzling day. A barred owl blinked, hooted an adieu to the night, and settled on a huge hemlock limb for a snooze. A raven sounded a raspy reveille. A gray squirrel responded from the sugarbush behind the cabin.

Stirring in my bunk, I was only vaguely aware of all that until a spaniel nose was poked into my ear. Whimpering for me to hurry, Chips panted impatiently at the door while I dressed.

Outside there was an air of autumn, accentuated by blushes of color in the maples. The pump handle, cold and shiny with dew, complained shrilly as I put it to work. A pot of iron-flecked water for coffee was a start, but breakfast required further planning. How about a skillet full of speckled trout?

I hadn't really intended to stop at the cabin. My major mission was musky fishing, and there are better musky waters than the south fork of the Flambeau River. However, when "No Vacancy" signs appeared at every motel enroute to Woodruff, I'd detoured westward, arriving at the old camp just before dark.

I hadn't stopped for groceries, for there is usually something left in the cupboard. What I'd found was some coffee, aged oatmeal and damp soda crackers. Chips' supper had looked better than mine.

But breakfast would be different. I knew that brook trout had already begun their fall journeys to the headwaters. So, with the mud-spattered truck in four-wheel drive, I headed for a dirt road which winds through the big blowdown -- a tract of forest felled by a violent storm in the summer of '77.

Parking at a bridge, I saw that lush growth had already hidden much of the destruction. However, toppled alders bordering the creek were still a terrible tangle for a man carrying a fishing rod.

I hadn't much time, and I was hungry, so I didn't delay. An ultralight spinning rod was handy. I tied a tarnished "O" size gold French spinner to the four-pound line and flipped it into the dark, chuckling water near the bridge.

There is something about the rush of wild water which makes one's blood course to keep pace; something about wild places which transports one back in time. I retrieved the lure, flipped it out again; watched it whirl and wobble back.

A flash from the undercut bank ended my reverie. The little rod danced and the reel buzzed briefly as I tugged a jeweled fish ashore. The nine-inch brookie was firm and cold in my grip as I broke its neck. I slipped it onto a limber stringer, cut from a streamside branch.

As I moved downstream, Chips was casting to and fro. A woodcock flushed on twittering wings, quickening my pulse again.

One of the joys of stream fishing is that you are wandering in the woods as you wade the currents or walk the banks. I could see that the ferns were now dappled brown. I watched a hummingbird hover in the yellow jewelweeds.

Just three small trout hung from my stick stringer when I turned back toward the road. I had hoped for more, but they would suffice.

A ruffed grouse, dark and bedraggled looking, flushed from under the dew-laden ferns. Five others followed as Chips nosed them out. A brood no doubt. Minutes later, the dog jumped a somewhat larger grouse, probably the hen.

As we approached the road I glimpsed a deer bounding away, white flag waving over wide russet haunches. I saw no antlers, although it was a big enough animal to be wearing a lot of them.

Then, on the way back to the cabin, I stopped to pick the last of what must have been a bumper crop of blackberries. I collected perhaps two cupfuls in my hat.

So there were those sweet, tart berries, poached trout, crackers and steamy coffee for breakfast, and a gray dawn had turned into a golden day.

And I wondered if anyone could feel more satisfied dining in the finest restaurant while closing a million dollar deal.

(09/24/78)

FALL FIRE

The fall fire is in the woods.

It begins with faint flickers in the sumacs along the streams; then blazes across the uplands. Flames leap from crown to crown in the maples while ferns below become scorched and brown.

First in the fiery maples, then in the yellow glow of aspens, then in the russet gleam of oaks, it rides the north wind, spreading southward, coals sizzling in a cold rain, rekindling under the autumn sun.

Spring, it is said, travels northward at the rate of 15 miles per day. Autumn follows no such orderly procession.

Like embers carried on a gusty wind, its colors fall on new tinder each night. The morning mists rise like smoke, revealing a hundred, a thousand, new fires in the hills

The north woods are aflame, and sparks are already falling in our very own back yards.

Say goodbye to summer. Its cremation is at hand.

(09/28/62)

OCTOBER

WARNING LIGHTS

The warning lamps are lit. Amber in the tamaracks, red in the maples.

The alarms are sounding. The call of geese wavering in the north wind. Jays rallying. Catbirds crying.

What is there in the keen scent of an October morning that so quickens the pulse, tingles the spine? A dim remembering, perhaps. The smell of danger in the air. A signal to prepare for winter or retreat.

And what is it that renders so pure the last lilting note of the meadowlark, the bright blue of asters, the frosty essence of mints in the marsh? It is that life never seems so dear as when it is departing.

October is a time of goodbyes, but it's a fine feast and farewell party while it lasts.

Rocket bursts of color are exploding in the hardwoods, swirling through smoky mists of morning, streaming across the sky at sunset.

And seldom has the banquet table been more burdened.

Bright purple umbels of elder bushes still hold sweet, shriveling fruit. The birds, for all they've tried, have been unable to consume the bounty of berries in our woods.

Raccoons are reaping the last wild cherries from the highest limbs before descending to gorge on grapes. Pheasants are fattening on grasshoppers in fallow fields. Grouse cluck contentedly in the hawthorns. Cedar branches are blue with berries, beckoning waxwings.

Squirrels scarcely know which way to turn amid a rain of acorns and the plopping of hickory and hazel nuts. The woodchuck is waddling fat as it heads for its den. Deer and bears are plump, sleek in thick, winter coats.

For now the woodlands are fluttering, rustling, scampering with vibrant life. But the somber signs are growing:

An empty nest. A tufted caterpillar tumbling with a leaf plucked by the wind. Thistle down rising. Pelting showers of jewelweed seeds when a rabbit brushes by.

This is the time of the bittersweet. The bittersweet time. It is when cobwebs, sagging with dew, shimmer in the rising sun like tattered remnants of the morning mist. It is when closed gentians shine cool blue beneath the fiery holly berries.

The silence falls slowly. One morning the excited chatter of the chipmunks is no longer heard along the path. Another day, the doves will no longer flush from the willows on singing wings. The wood ducks will be gone from the creek. The woodchuck will stay in bed.

October's invitation is now. Go early and stay as long as you can, for the party must end all too soon.

And November will cry cold tears.

(10/02/69)

THE FEVER

An ailing friend called yesterday, and I immediately perceived by the sound of his voice that he was recovering, if not completely cured, of a nasty malady which had nearly brought him down.

What made me even happier was the assurance that my diagnosis and prescription had been correct. What the man had needed was a new woodcock gun.

I was with him at the onset of the symptoms earlier this fall. We had hunted hard and long for woodcock, slogging and crashing through all manner of wild, wet cover. At last we'd found a scattering of the elusive birds. I was fortunate to bag four of them, while he struggled to shoulder and swing his gun in the dense growth.

Back at the cabin that night, my friend hefted the light, open-bored double barrel I'd been using. He pointed it; swung it, and then scowled at his old pumpgun. That's how it started.

"Don't get rid of that old gun," I warned, noticing that a tic had developed in his left eye. He could shoot that pumpgun all right. It has proved deadly on various other species, It just wasn't the best choice for shooting timberdoodles. Sort of like a golfer using a 7-iron on the green.

The virus had spread by the time we met again last week. I couldn't help but notice that he was sniveling, drooling, and chewing on the lapels of his hunting coat.

"I saw this sweet little double," he babbled. "It's too expensive, but it's a 20, with a straight grip, 26-inch barrels, bored improved cylinder and modified..."

To cure his ague, the price he mentioned sounded like a bargain, medical expenses being what they are these days.

"Buy it!" I prescribed. I told him that such a gun would be a good investment. And beside, look at all the money he could save by eating woodcock instead of expensive hamburger.

Still uncertain, almost delirious, he tottered home and took to his bed. His wife tried to save him. She even rubbed Vicks on his chest. But the end seemed near.

Finally, summoning his remaining strength, he sprang up and ran, reeking, to the sports shop. He called me from there. Of course, he had bought the gun.

Despite the fact that he is also destined to miss a goodly number of woodcock with the new gun, anyone who has been similarly affected will recognize this as a happy ending.

But alas, the virus is recurrent and takes various forms. Sometimes it can only be combatted with a trap gun. Another time, a 10 gauge magnum is required. In severe cases, treatments may include engraving or gold inlays, a selective trigger and automatic ejectors.

Just as serious are the types which respond only to a 30-06 or an outboard motor, or which demand generous applications of rods, reels and lures.

Which reminds me: I've concluded that the ideal musky rod should be built on a stiff, one-piece blank, six feet or a bit longer, with a two-handed grip and offset handle. Since seeing one like that recently, I've had a troublesome twitch in my right arm.

I wonder if anyone sells medical insurance for problems like that.

(10/07/78)

FALL RAIN

Raindrops tapping of the roof of an empty martin house. Rain sizzling in fiery sumacs along a swollen stream. Drenched robins huddled in the hollies. Ducks dabbling in flooded fields.

Since the rains began, autumn scenes have been brushed on a sodden, gray canvas. The colors have run; faded. Wet winds have tugged blotchy, brown foliage from the hickories and launched drab fleets of willow leaves into the creek.

Fall, it seems, has turned from those drab reflections in rain-dimpled lakes and is slinking dejectedly away.

But not so fast. Some colors still cling to the palette. Enough to daub the maples with soft yellows and pale pinks. Enough to splash an oak's crown with purple. Enough to paint a pastel montage on a hillside, even in the morning mists.

And there is more, much more, to autumn than painted foliage. There are meadowlarks singing farewells as sweet as their greetings in spring. There are flocks of flickers feeding in the clearings, clouds of blackbirds scudding over the marshes, formations of geese clamoring across the sky.

A turtle, shell varnished by rain, is toddling towards a winter retreat in the mud of a nearby pond. A squirrel, scampering noiselessly over sodden leaves, is tirelessly storing provisions for the long wait to spring. A speckled trout, tailing against the creek's quick current, senses that spawning time in nigh.

From such as they, we learn that autumn is not simply an end, but a beginning. In the flutter of passing wings, in the chuckle of mallards in puddled stubblefields, in the metered tapping of a wind-worried leaf against a bough, a heartbeat can be heard. Such is the pulse of the seasons, palpitating, ebbing, quickening.

But sometimes nature seems to miss a beat. Enough now, of October showers. We'll welcome them back in spring.

(10/09/65)

OCTOBER WINGS

Blue sky scrawled with wavering lines of geese. Green meadow glittering with golden butterflies. Hawks soaring high; circling south.

October must be passing through.

It rides on wings, does October. Birds flutter through our woods like leaves swirling in autumn winds. Some linger. Few will stay.

There are flickers in the field. Robins have banded along the brushy bank. Warblers have paused for small talk amid holly branches. Their plumage pales now against the yellow lights in the swamp maples; the fires dancing in the dogwood and sumac.

A fat brown spider binding a blue dragonfly to a goldenrod with silver thread. Acorns plopping to a carpet of mottled hickory leaves. Closed gentians glowing at the edge of the swamp.

Such were the small happenings along our path this day.

And when a cloud of redwings came to roost at dusk, the somber marsh burst into song.

Soon, too soon, the quiet will return. And winter.

For October rides on restless wings.

(10/11/68)

THE OLD SHACK

Wide Slough, Wis. -- A raccoon's paws are rasping the side of the shack. Old Ringtail is muttering because he can't find the source of inviting smells adrift in the night breeze. Then the masked prowler is silent. He doubtless is studying the problem like any practiced burglar. By climbing a big maple, he could walk along a large limb and drop onto the roof; then feast on the ducks we've placed there to cool.

I'm too full of stew to take my feet off the table, but my harmonica is within reach. A spirited rendition of "There's No Place Like Home" rends the silence of the swamp. The raccoon flees, but a barred owl gets into the spirit of the song. One of us is off key.

Bob Dreis shoves the door open to clear the little room of smoke from the balky wood range and our pipes. Leaves rustle nervously outside for a moment. A mouse scurries through the door and across the floor. Night seeps in silently behind it.

"You're not taking many notes today, " Bob observes drowsily. But who needs a pencil to help remember such a night?

We lack a wick for the oil lamp. One improvised of rag produces only sputterings and smoke, so now there is only the flickering yellow light of a candle in the shack. Just beyond the open door though, is a crystal chandelier of stars. As one gazes, the stars come closer, until we are among them. The lights and fumes of cities veil the wonders of the night sky. Only at sea, or at a distance from civilization, do we see the real brilliance of the heavens.

Men seldom speak of why they come to places like this. We assure each other that we came to hunt ducks; that we dragged the canoe across beaver dams and fallen trees and slogged through clinging mud just to bag a few birds. But that is only a part of it. The shack is a symbol; a haven.

It is a shabby shelter. There is no television, no radio, no telephone; no road. The furnishings are few and crude, but weary bones won't complain about bunks made of unyielding boards.

Many memories are huddled under the tarpaper roof. On the walls are records of catches during the days when this was a trapper's shanty. Scribbled there too, are scores kept of hunts in other seasons.

I am remembering too, a sign I once saw over the door of another cabin in the woods. It said "The Clinic." Anyone who has felt the therapy of such a hideaway knows how appropriate that is.

A beaver is slapping its tail on the surface of a distant slough. The sound echoes through these broad bottomlands bounding the Chippewa River. The fire and the candle have both burned low. It is time to close the door and go to bed.

Swirling mists will shroud the shack when we arise before dawn. Then the stars will be out of focus and the owl's voice will be muffled by the fog.

But at this moment the night reveals stars, and truths, with a clarity which moves a man to peace.

(10/12/63)

A BLUEBIRD'S ADIEU

Geese chorusing across a steely sky. Frost on the roof. Ice in the dog's dish. Blackbirds noisily discussing departure plans as they flutter over the misty creek.

How swiftly autumn fades, shivering, shriveling, when the north wind whets the edge of day.

On the hill behind the house, a huge maple sheds its few remaining leaves. Bright yellow, like shards of summer's sunbeams falling brittle and broken to earth. Sparse, russet foliage rattles on oak limbs. Hickories look ragged and forlorn, and gleams of gold in the swamp tamaracks confirm that autumn is very old.

The wind has torn away the leafy shutters which screen our view from the house in summer. Now, where only glints of the creek were visible, we again see it winding through tattered ranks of cattails. Other things once hidden by foliage are also revealed: An oriole's nest in the maple, a squirrel's retreat in an oak.

A bird is perched atop the bluebird house. It might be a sparrow seeking snug winter quarters. However, a flash of color and a few notes of song reveal its true identity.

"Cheerily! Cheerily!" the male bird whistles. He then flutters to a nearby limb and sings again before flying away.

As usual, the bluebirds raised two broods in that birdhouse this year. Then, as is their custom, they disappeared for a time, to take a well-earned late summer rest. But always, they come back, if but briefly, as autumn wanes.

Sometimes there is the whole family, sometimes only the parent pair, seeming to seek reassurance that their summer home is still there and will be waiting, come spring.

Collar turned up, fists clenched in pockets, I watch the bright songster join his mate and disappear into the cold, gray sky.

Juncos flit in the dogwoods. Jays scold. Chickadees call. The woods are full of winter sounds, but the bluebird has promised that he, and spring, will find their way back again.

It is a warming thought as I scuff back up the frosty path, those parting notes echoing:

Cheerily.

(10/19/76)

TOO MUCH STUFF

I was carrying the fifth armload of equipment out to the truck when Lorraine, holding the door, made an observation I'd heard several times before:

"My father never needed all that stuff," my good wife said. "He'd just put on his coat and take his gun or fishing pole and go."

I waited for the clincher. It's not polite to walk away when somebody's telling you something for your own good:

"And in those days, we lived on what he brought back," she reminded me...

Outside, I pondered over the growing pile of gear. What could be dispensed with? How about all those boots? Leather birdshooters, rubber pacs, hipboots. Hmmmm. 'Good thing I checked. I'd better thrown in the chest high waders, too.

Fishing tackle? Those two musky rods are the absolute minimum. One is for bucktails; the other's for plugs. The spinning outfit is for walleyes, of course, and that ultra-light rig is included in anticipation of some fine fall bluegill and crappie action. Oh, all those tackle boxes? It's just simpler to have one for each kind of fishing.

The guns then? Well, the .22 is for squirrels, that heavy old pumpgun is for waterfowl and the double barrel is for grouse and woodcock. Yes, I know that's quite an assortment of ammunition, but you need to have light loads and heavy loads; fine shot, coarse shot, steel shot...

And of course I need all those jackets. Fall weather is so variable that one needs everything from rain parka to lightweight vest to insulated coat. Then too, you need bright colors for safety while birdhunting and camouflage patterns for the duck blind. That assortment of caps just goes along with the jackets.

Sure, I have marsh skis, and an olive drab canoe with matching pushpole and paddles, and enough decoys to fill it to the gunwales.

Some of my reasons for lugging all that stuff around seem valid enough. Ducks and grouse and fish aren't as easy to get as they used to be. In some cases it's because they're scarcer, but it's also because they're smarter. And that's a fact.

We used to catch limits of walleyes below the Mississippi River wing dams by dangling gobs of nightcrawlers on coarse, black lines. Try that today. Some of today's sophisticated fish are spooked by monofilament line so fine that I can hardly see it myself.

Bass used to be easy game for plugs skittered along weedbeds with long canepoles, and creek trout were suckers for manure worms impaled on black enameled hooks.

The more our ruffed grouse have been hunted, the warier they've become. And just any old duck decoys won't do anymore either. Flocks will pass right over and set wings at someone else's spread of giant blocks which -- except for size -- look more like ducks than they do.

But look, I really have drawn the line. I do have some oversized decoys, but nothing like some I've seen lately. Just a bit bigger and they'll be able to put oarlocks on them and use them as skiffs.

I don't have a hunting blind that looks like a goose, with wings which flap open when I want to shoot. I've never bought any plastic facsimiles of ear corn to attract waterfowl, with a matching poncho printed with a corn pattern.

I'm not flying kites that look like geese, and not one of my decoys is a radio-controlled model which will swim to and fro and even (it is advertised) retrieve ducks.

All of the equipment I do have is used, but I wonder if that's the real test of whether or not it's necessary. One of these days, maybe I'll just pull on a shabby old coat and set out with the dog and the old single shot, and see.

Keep it simple. It sounds appealing. But I'm sure glad I won't have to live on what I bring back.

(10/31/78)

NOVEMBER

NOVEMBER FLAGS

Clouds of blackbirds. Hawks hurrying. Brief blizzards of snow geese gusting across the sky. The warning flags are flying. Winter is on the way.

But our woodpiles are stacked high, potatoes and carrots and beets are dug, squash are picked and the snowblower is primed and poised. So now there's time to kick through the leaves along the path to the creek; to sit on a stump, sniffing the keen air and reflecting on current events around our country home.

Such as milkweed pods exploding into sparkling plumes at frosty dawns. And salamanders hiding under rotted logs in the leaf-strewn woods. And raccoons harvesting wild grapes on the hillside.

And then there are those wooly worms going thither and yon, traveling at a scurrying pace for caterpillars. They appear unable to predict what kind of weather is in store. Some wear broad black bands which, according to folklore, foretell a severe winter. Others are mostly brown. However, one was found snuggled under a sun-warmed stone. That might be a clue as to what that wooly worm expects, for its kind commonly snoozes in stubble fields all winter.

Larvae of the night-flying tiger moths, wooly worms don't spin their cocoons until spring. Their hair, which contains an irritating substance, provides some protection. Resourceful skunks, however, roll the hairs off before eating the caterpillars. So much for nature's strategies.

By the time November appears on the horizon, gray and grumpy-looking, most creatures, large and small, have made their preparations.

These days the wood-splitting maul reveals big carpenter ants huddled in oaken caverns, drowsy; body juices already primed with antifreeze.

The chipmunk has the pantry of its den packed with acorns and seeds, while the rotund raccoon has stored fat to keep it warm and nourished as it waits through winter's worst.

The birds, most of them, have looked to the mysterious maps they carry in their genes, setting courses for sundry exotic places: the Jamaican jungle, the Yucatan Peninsula, the mountains of Peru.

Some robust looking robins are still bouncing around in the backyard, but the songbird tide has ebbed in our woods. Those tireless tree swallows which summered with us. The rose-breasted grosbeaks, orioles and tanagers. Wood thrush and ovenbird; veery and vireo. All those have left. But memories of their exuberant dawn concerts still echo in the woods.

The bluebirds were among the last to leave. Despite a late start, the parent pair raised two broods. One October day they all lined up on a fence wire to have their census taken. Eleven of them. That was something to sing about. Then they too were gone.

Winter birds are already filling the voids. Most of them -- cardinals and bluejays, nuthatches and chickadees, woodpeckers and goldfinches -- are really year-round residents.

They're not backyard birds when there is abundant food elsewhere. but now they come again, vibrant life and color fluttering from the bleak woods to offerings of sunflower seeds and suet.

Later there will be others: Purple finches, juncos; creepers. And perhaps evening grosbeaks will arrive when winter shadows are long against the snow.

They're lengthening fast, those shadows. The gold of summer's sunrise has turned to brass -- bright, but cold. Summer's fiery sunsets are faint memories in the pale glow that ends a November day.

Now, as thin gray clouds flutter like pennants in the quickening north wind, one sees that sails have been reefed in the swamp. Insecurely anchored in bogs, the tamaracks will meet winter's blows bare-masted.

I can see no farther from my perch on that stump, but the signs all around are clear:

November has arrived. Winter will be here soon.

(11/02/79)

MAKING WOOD

Autumn's last embers have been doused by cold rains. Maples stand naked, shivering in a raw wind. Like tatters of wet, brown paper, leaves still flap soggily in the oaks.

But even as the fires outside sizzled and died, a new one was kindled in our fireplace.

Some men need a woodlot. I am one of those. And a woodlot needs a fireplace, for time and wind constantly cull the old and the weak.

Windfalls furnish all of our firewood, because, as long as a hollow tree remains standing it does not have an empty heart. Squirrels, woodpeckers, wood ducks, owls and raccoons. Those are some of the many left homeless if we maintain too neat a woods.

A gusty summer made much work for ax and saw this year -- and late autumn is the time. The mosquitoes are gone. And one can work in shirtsleeves, barehanded, because there is plenty of warmth in an ax handle kept in motion.

There is a glad ring in the blade on a frosty morning, and it seems to invite the company of birds. Curiosity, and a bounty of bugs within the wood, bring some of them close.

A downy woodpecker clings to a hickory's shaggy bark, watching. It is waiting to explore the contents of an ancient oak trunk just dissected by the saw.

Nor do our chickens show any fear of the ax. They crowd close as the oak chunks are split, clucking in contentment as they snap up the ants and grubs hidden within.

Migrant robins and golden crowned kinglets flit through the dogwoods. Cardinals flash through the holly bushes. The juncos are back.

A sleepy chipmunk scurries from a hollow snag to escape the gnawing saw. The dog gives chase. A nervous squirrel chatters from a distant oak. One can follow its flight through swaying branches as it races for refuge in a hollow hickory.

Simple skills are needed to build a pile of wood. Experience teaches which pieces will split readily; which should be stacked for seasoning. Trail, and error, sometimes must be employed to test a stubborn chunk for a weakness which will yield to ax or wedge.

Hard work, yes, but there is deep satisfaction when a man views his own woodpile. It is an old feeling, I suppose. There is a sense of security against the coming cold; a feeling of accomplishment no less gratifying than the completion of a painting or composing of a sonnet.

In an orderly life, there should be a time for composing, and a time for chopping wood.

It is a good weariness a man earns as he heaps his woodpile higher. It is mingled with thoughts of sparks leaping up the chimney, the scent of woodsmoke, of children toasting marshmallows and the dog lazing before a flickering fire.

The woods glisten now with rain. Soon they will be cold, white and still.

But our hearth will offer warmth and dancing light, like sunbeams glancing through summer's leaves.

It seems some men need a woodlot. And I am one of those.

(11/03/67)

THE SWAN SONG

The sound first comes in bits and tatters, soft and silvery, like the last of the thistle's down tossed in the north wind. Like village church bells heard aboard a ship far at sea. Like echoes from another time; another world.

The first muted notes prompt ears to remember and eyes to search the sky. The swans are flying.

Where are they? How is it that they can fly unseen across a cloudless sky? Why does the sound swirl from here, then there, like the skirlings of ghostly bagpipes?

There then. High, high over the horizon. Sparkling like a handful of snowflakes cast across the sky. As they come nearer, even the bustling dog pauses at my side, seemingly under the spell. Now they are a fleet of shining sails billowing across a pale blue sea, great wings beating to the rhythm of that strange, wild song. Eastbound, their course set for the climbing sun.

Then gone. And with them, what was left of autumn.

Tundra swans do not predict the change of seasons. They declare them. Unlike the uncertainties of geese, which spring and fall are apt to rush the season, there is a finality in the flight of swans.

So there seems a new chill in the morning air as, hands in pockets, collar turned up, I scuff through brittle leaves to the margins of the marsh. Ragged cattails shower frost as the dog bounds amid them, looks back questioningly; then leaps high. A rooster pheasant rockets away, a riot of color as he climbs over the tamaracks. He is still cackling with indignation as he sets wings and glides across the creek.

The creek looks cold, gray, reflecting scenes as somber as my thoughts. A jacksnipe flies from the creek. It has been drawn there by a margin of half-frozen mud. The snipe's rotund cousin, the woodcock, has already left us. The snipe will soon follow.

More swans now. Some flocks in perfect V formations, others rippling in long, curving lines, like white-capped waves hurrying to the horizon.

They were long known as whistling swans, but why I cannot say. I have listened to them since boyhood, have spent time at the remote Arctic ponds where they nest and visited their winter communes, and I have never heard one whistle. Rather, their sound is a hooting, a whooping, a trumpeting. Hollow, off key, yet strangely musical. They are vocal birds whether on water or in the air, and they can be heard for miles.

Sometimes the swans are confused with snow geese, which are much smaller birds with black wingtips. Swans have all-white wings spanning six feet or more, and their motion is even more graceful than that of geese. Long neck outstretched, black feet trailing, the swan's flight is fluid.

As befits such a large, fast-flying machine, the swan travels in rarified air, and for long distances between landings. The bird winters mostly along the Atlantic coast from Chesapeake Bay southward to North Carolina. That explains why its course often turns eastward when it reaches our latitudes.

Although white as snow, a creature of the Arctic and a bearer of winter, I think the swans must have a strong affinity for the sun, which lingers long in the sky during most of their stay in the Arctic. When swans migrate, it is usually on clear days. Otherwise, they will fly above the clouds, where the sun blazes bright.

So we can be assured of this: When the sun heads north again, that same old music will swell across the sky. It is the swan song of two seasons. Today it meant that autumn is no more. When next we hear it, winter will be done.

(11/20/78)

ONE MORE TRY

Brule, Wis. -- Fishing seems such a gentle madness, but its grip is steel.

What else could snatch a man from a cozy bunk, tug him out into a frosty dawn and push him into a freezing stream? What else could compel men to splash along the Brule River while snow cascades from sagging evergreens; and clammy mists creep in from Lake Superior.

And what else could have struck a trance in the big man who waded near, dancing over slippery rocks, just as we were finishing our shore lunch?

"It's the last day," he muttered softly. He spoke it as a sort of requiem. His gaze remained distant, even as we exchanged information on the baits we had tried.

He had taken two trout -- a steelhead and a brown -- on tiny sacks of trout spawn. We told him that we had the right bait, but no fish. We asked to take a picture of his. He nodded. He would show us where he had cached his catch, but he would not be photographed and his name must not be known. We agreed, not questioning.

It is probable that the man's employer thought he was selling rubber wrenches to hospital janitors -- or whatever he was supposed to be doing at that moment. But the grip of the river was unrelenting. The man with the faraway gaze would have been worthless anywhere else on the last day of the season, so the deceived boss was losing nothing.

Fishing is a deceitful business. One fibs to the fish with barbed baits and fraudulent food, exaggerates about the ones which get away; lies about the lure that tricked a lunker. So we became co-conspirators with the big man in waders whom we did not know, yet knew very well.

He led us through the woods to where he had hidden a four-pound steelhead -- a metallic rainbow shining on the snow -- and a boldly-spotted brown trout perhaps half a pound lighter. Bright pink beads of spawn spilled onto the snow as the brown was lifted toward the camera. The fisherman moved quickly to catch the eggs in a plastic bag. They would be bait next spring.

The anonymous angler was the fourth fisherman we had met, and the first to have a fish. Two others were seen in the afternoon as we drifted and paddled farther downriver. One had taken a small steelhead. Too small. But for him, as for us, just being there was enough. There was beauty and tranquility along the river. And the chance that wild excitement could explode at any moment.

We had slipped the canoe into the river at the Highway 13 bridge. Larry Denston of Brule and this reporter were casting and paddling. Jim Meyer alternately fished and shot film.

Jim was making a movie. He had hoped for footage of shimmering trout dancing in icy spray against a snowy backdrop. The setting was perfect, but the fish hadn't read the script.

We paused at eddies and drifted spawn sacks through the currents. We worked the ice-edged shore with artificial lures. Hours and miles passed. Feet and fingers became stinging cold. Drifting chunks of ice sometimes tugged at our lines, causing instants of hope.

"I'm really enjoying this," Jim said.

"Me too," I answered.

And the madness was that we meant it.

Darkness deepened. Fog thickened. Rapids became only blurs of snow-capped boulders in the murk. We bounced and scraped onward until we met a sheet of ice which stretched from shore to shore. It yielded for a few feet; then stopped us cold.

Our car awaited near the river mouth, but solid ice blocked the Brule for a mile or more above the lake. So we left the canoe high on a steep bank and hiked for the road, much encumbered with gear, but glad for the exercise which pumped warmth back into fingers and toes.

We philosophized. We were not sorry that we had lost the gamble. It had been worth one more try. This was not the first time that winter had frozen our hopes on the Brule. It probably would not be the last.

More snow sifted down as we walked. The wind told us that winter had come to stay. But in early April, before those flakes melted, we would return. The big man -- and the others we'd met -- they would be back too. For once an angler has felt the spell, the season opening is an invitation not to be denied. It is a beckoning finger, on an iron hand.

(11/18/65)

OPENING DAY

Some wonder what it is that lures legions of hunters from snug beds to chilly deer stands on opening day. There is, of course, the expectation, the dream of meeting a mighty buck. But there is more. Much more. So come along and see.

There was that spell of silence before the first glimmer of day. Reluctant to break it, I paused at the old farm lane, listening.

Not a sound. Was it possible that I'd have this place all to myself? I held my watch to the light of the moon, still high and bright. It was 5:55 a.m. Forty minutes and half a mile to go...

Quilted with snow, fields twinkled as if reflecting the stars. I crunched softly up a hill, along the woods, down another slope; then along a brushy fence row to an aged oak. Because it stood directly on the fenceline, the tree had been spared when the now-fallow fields were cleared. For many decades it had done duty as a sturdy fencepost. This morning it was also my backrest.

Some deer hunters are dedicated to old, familiar stands. And with good reason. They are places which have produced in the past. Others of us are more restless. I enjoy the familiarity and camaraderie of the old northwoods deer camp, but I also like to try new places.

This time I was on a tract of state land in southeastern Wisconsin, and my stand was not one which would be picked at first glance. There was no well-worn deer run within sight. However, I knew it to be on an escape route for a fine buck. While pheasant hunting, I had twice seen

115

him sulking along the fenceline.

At 6:10 a. m. a screech owl wailed tremulously. A pheasant rooster crowed. Stars were dimming in the graying sky. The waiting was about to end. And to begin...

A mouse rustled in the snow near my feet. The movement was so amplified in the stillness that it sounded like a stampede. A nuthatch started prying bits of loose bark from a nearby tree. It sounded like someone tearing shingles from a house.

"Ba-LOOM!" The first shot rolled across the hills. I judged it to be a mile or more away. This was shotgun country and the bellow of those big-mouthed guns carries much farther than the heavy slugs they fling.

Another distant gun joined in. And another. For some, the season had started 10 minutes early. Those minutes passed, and five more. The morning chill was seeping slowly to my toes, my fingers, my spine. I was tempted to move a bit. But wait...wait...here they come!

Two deer bounded into view, slowed to a walk, stopped; looked around. Only 30 yards away. An easy shot.

My pulse returned to normal. It was a pair of yearlings. I had bigger hopes for my tag. The youngsters were not greatly alarmed. One of them pawed at something its nose had detected beneath the snow. It began to feed. But the other remained alert. It did a nervous little dance, swaying side to side. Suddenly then, tails up, both bounded lightly over the hill.

At the edge of a woods some 200 yards away, a hunter appeared, aglow in blaze-orange garb. He was still waiting there when, 15 minutes later, two deer emerged from a nearby marsh. They were a large doe with a late fawn, so small that it looked like a dog following at heel. They started to cross the field. I stepped behind the tree when I saw the other hunter raising his gun. His shots were still echoing as I saw both deer disappear over the hill.

During the next hour, other hunters appeared. I saw a father giving last-minute instructions to his son before they parted at the hilltop. I watched the boy start out on a solo hike, excitement evident in his stride, head turning alertly as he marched toward the next woodlot. It stirred memories.

Day had dawned rosy, crisp and still, but a chilling wind had risen with the sun. My jacket's bulging game pocket yielded a small vacuum bottle of steaming coffee, two thick cheese and sausage sandwiches made with home-made bread and a piece of freshly-baked spice cake. That girl I married knows how to equip a man for deer hunting. I was warm again.

Five geese flew over. Big honkers. The season was still open. I should remember to load the gun with fine shot as soon as I tagged that buck, just in case some more flew over. Such are the fantasies of a man on a deer stand.

Now I could see three more gunners skirting the marsh. They were following a dog. Pheasant hunters. More than two hours had passed, a long time for this restless woods wanderer to keep vigil in one place.

No nearby shooting had been heard, except for those shots at the doe and fawn. Apparently the buck had chosen his hideout well this day.

More geese were flying over as I hiked back to the truck. The sun was shining. The snow was softening. Many miles and hours of hunting lay ahead. I looked forward to them. It would be a pity, wouldn't it, to have the hunt end so soon?

The season was off to a fine start indeed.

(11/25/75)

THE ERMINE

Ingram, Wis.-- If the other hunter was aware of us, he gave no sign of it. One glance told that he was out for blood and wanted no nonsense from intruders. So we simply watched in quiet fascination.

The hunter was an ermine -- the little weasel which in winter wears the robe of kings. Pure white, except for its beady eyes and black-tipped tail, it darted through the brown woods like intermittent flashes of light. It poked into burrows and streaked up trees to explore their hollows. It was the purposeful, relentless search of a hungry killer.

Don Williams and I had been solo hunting for deer most of the day. We had met in the woods only minutes earlier, and were discussing a route for hunting back toward camp, when the ermine appeared.

It scurried along the old logging trail, streaking in and out of windfalls, stopping to sniff at every possible hideout for its prey. It came ever closer, seeming oblivious to us, until we might have touched it with a gun barrel.

Virtually at my feet, the ermine dived into the hollow of a fallen tree. Two deer mice darted out another hole in the trunk. They looked frightened and confused. One hid under a pile of sticks. The other scampered a few feet farther and froze, nearly invisible against the dry leaves.

The ermine reappeared, excited, eyes shining. It ran to and fro for a moment or two; then dived under the sticks. There were two tiny squeaks of terror. Then the ermine emerged with the mouse hanging limply from its immaculate, blood-free jaws.

The mouse was quickly cached under the sticks and the hunt continued. The ermine started searching in the wrong direction, but the second mouse panicked. It scurried up a small sapling. The ermine's eyes caught the movement. He turned back, combing the area carefully, seemingly in vain. We thought that the mouse had escaped.

However, an instant later we saw a white streak in the sapling and heard another tiny death cry pierce that quiet corner of the woods. Like the first, the mouse had been killed instantly with a bite through the back of the head.

Satisfied that there were no more mice in the immediate area, the ermine carried its second prize under the fallen tree for a feast. We did not disturb it. The killer had committed no crime.

In a world divided into predator and prey, the mice had met the natural fate of their kind. Indeed, in the absence of killers to control their numbers, the prey species usually meet worse ends.

We moved on then, again intent on finding deer.

For man is one of the predators. And, if you think about it, that is something to be thankful for.

(11/26/64)

THE HUNT

Hawkins, Wis. -- Silence settles over the woods as I stop at the edge of the big spruce swamp. The faint crunch of my boots still echoes in my ears, I can sense forest creatures holding their breaths, waiting for the next footfall.

Outwait them then. There is no way I can approach a deer unaware this morning. The sharp temperature drop during the night has crusted the snow and left every stem and twig fuzzy with frost.

So listen. First there is the labored wingbeat of a raven on its morning rounds, wings swishing and rasping like the corduroy knickers I loathed as a schoolboy. The bird is making its morning patrol at low altitude, missing nothing.

Gawking at the scene below, the raven utters a guttural comment. I suspect that it refers to my resplendent array in the uniform of the season. I agree. Although the ragged-looking raven is hardly the Beau Brummel of the northwoods, he's a sight prettier than an unshaven deer hunter peering out from a bundle of blaze-orange garb.

Fifteen minutes later there's a rustle in an old maple behind me. A big gray squirrel, as rotund and furry as a teddy bear, has emerged from a hollow. It descends and bounds away almost soundlessly.

Now treetops are sparkling against the bright, blue sky. When the wind sighs, frost crystals swirl down in brief, dazzling blizzards. The sun has climbed above the tallest hemlock and is peeking down through the spruces. The snow is softening.

Time to move. Cautiously. Step on nothing you can step over or around. Stop often. Look everywhere, including back over your shoulder.

There is an old logging camp clearing just ahead. A ruffed grouse explodes from the berry brambles there. Wait. There goes another. Spooky birds. Neither would have offered a chance with the shotgun. Who says that they are too vulnerable to hunters in winter?

There is much history in these old clearings. Tread carefully around the brambles and through the tall, tawny weeds woven above the snow, for they hide the crumbled remains of a well, dug deep through jumbled rock and unyielding hardpan by men who were harder still.

The shambles of a log cabin sag sadly in one corner of this clearing. Originally built by the loggers, it served a gang of deer hunters for decades. Just stand in the gaping doorway and listen.

If only those creaking walls could speak. What stories they could tell about the days when the big pines fell; about those deer hunts in the cutover in the years that followed.

They must have been quite a crew. Bunks for 16. Benches around a roughhewn table. And one rocking chair. That was for the camp ramrod, no doubt.

A few huge, charred stumps remain nearby as memorials to those days. And there is still the dim outline of the ice road over which prodigious loads of logs were skidded. Stand quietly. Listen to the ring of axes, the cadence of crosscut saws; the creaking of a giant tree bending on its hinge before crashing to the ground.

To foil porcupines, this cabin had been skirted with corrugated iron. However, when the porkies concluded that the men weren't coming back, they just gnawed through the door. Then they gnawed the bunks, the rocking chair, everything. Even the aluminum kettles.

So now there are mice in the mattresses and holes in the roof. The big wood range has fallen through the rotting floor.

Time was when the cabin was in the midst of a huge deer herd. But eventually the hardwoods grew tall in the cutover country and the habitat shrank. Cruel winters came, and then there was overcrowding in the conifers where deer sought shelter and sustenance.

So the deer became scarcer and the old hunters older, and many of the younger ones followed the deer southward. Yet some stayed, or keep returning whenever they can. For us is deer season a reason, or is it just an excuse?

Move on. There are grosbeaks and chickadees and jays to keep me company. A red squirrel, uncommonly quiet, peers from a maple limb. Tundra swans wing over. High. Hurrying south.

Keep the edge of the swamp in sight while poking through the hardwoods on higher ground. Deer usually take this route, skirting the swamp. However, there are no fresh tracks this day. Into the swamp then, stepping from mossy hummock to hummock, careful not to trip in that watery tangle of roots and windfalls.

Dark water seeps from the swamp, gathering into a trickling stream which feeds Sullivan Creek, then Skinner Creek; then the South Fork of the Flambeau River. I kneel at a pool and sip water so cold that it leaves my tongue tingling; eyes blinking.

No deer have crossed the half-frozen swamp. Circle back to higher ground then. Take a breather and watch the trail.

I shot a fat forkhorn at this spot one year. I exactly recall every detail of how he bounded into view. And then, in my memory, is a parade of other deer.

It is a curious thing, how clearly they all come to mind. I can picture every deer I have ever tagged. I remember that buck I met head-on in the middle of a snowy cedar swamp so many years ago. And there was that six-pointer which watched me from behind a big boulder. And that one which leaped from a fallen treetop like a flushing grouse, not 10 feet away. And the time I tagged the monarch of these woods, the one the boys in camp had named "Old Curly."

But there is no buck on this trail today. They are not moving. 'Might as well keep moseying.

A porcupine, looking big as a fall bear cub, hitches up a big aspen as I approach. Halting about 10 feet from the ground, it watches stolidly as I walk by. Looking back from the next ridge, I can see the porky still clinging there, undecided.

Recent deer tracks punctuate the snow on the hardwood knolls farther south. There are coyote tracks there too. They angle across a frozen beaver pond beyond the ridge. It is a good place to wait as lengthening shadows stretch down one hill and up the next. It is going to be another frigid night. Not a flicker of a whitetail's flag has been seen. and it is time to start the long hike back to camp.

Some hunters have fared better this day. A few shots, muffled by distance, have been heard. Yet, even a record harvest will leave most hunters with nothing more than memories of days like this.

And for most of us, they are more than enough reason to try again.

(11/28/81)

THE LAST DAY

It was the last day of the deer season, and the woods seemed strangely hushed as the hunter paused to look and listen at the edge of a small pond.

A small brown spider was inching across the ice-skimmed pond. Its legs moved wearily, seemingly reluctantly. Life, as the spider knew it, was coming to an end.

Yet, just a fraction of an inch away, life still pulsed strongly. Along the very shore was a wavering border of dark water, barely an inch in width. It was there because the afternoon sky was clear and the dark earth had caught some warmth from the distant sun.

There, as if loathe to be sealed below, minnows were nosing up to the surface. There too, aquatic insects stroked rhythmically. And turtles. A snapper as big as a dish pan. A saucer-sized painted turtle.

When the hunter moved closer, the tread of his boots sent them away. As if through a frosted pane, they could be seen gliding deep into the murky depths, to the mud which would mother them for the next four months. The minnows darted away too, stirring brown leaves adrift in crystalline space. Only the insects remained unperturbed, unperturbable. They swam in unison on an endless, erratic course which kept bringing them back to that ribbon of open water. The spider walked oh-so-wearily above them all.

The hunter turned from the pond, his footsteps muffled by moss and a thin layer of moist snow, the first of the season. Dark water welled into his tracks until he gained slightly higher ground.

Back in the woods, wintergreen shone above the snow. The hunter picked a palmful of the gleaming red berries and savored their clean, refreshing flavor. It was a timeless place, and he did not know how long he stood there to watch and listen.

A chickadee flitted to a nearby branch and fluffed its feathers until it looked inflated; rotund. A snowshoe hare arrived. Its movements seemed ungainly, for only in speed do the hare's long legs give grace to the animal's motion, and only on deep snow are its big feet an advantage. The snowshoe was wearing its winter garb of white, except for tinges of gray remaining on the back of its neck. How conspicuous and uneasy the hare must have felt before the snow fell, the hunter mused. A raven croaked as it flew over, its wingbeats whooshing in the still, cold air.

Then bluejays began a clamor beyond the far edge of the pond, The hunter was instantly alert, for he knew the meaning. There is something in the jay's makeup which impels it to proclaim the furtive approach of any creature. The hunter had himself been the victim many times, while trying to stalk through the woods. He accepted it, albeit sometimes angrily, because it was a warning of wildlings to wildlings.

However, he had also often seen the birds betray a fox slinking by, or announce the approach of a skulking deer. That, it seemed to the hunter, was treachery. But he would accept the help, nonetheless.

The deer appeared near the pond's edge. It looked about nervously, neck extended, head close to the ground. The hunter raised his rifle and studied the deer through his telescopic sight. The jays had become silent.

The deer was a large doe, not the buck the hunter had been hoping for. He expelled the breath he'd been unaware of holding. The doe turned back into the woods and disappeared. A jay lit in a nearby tree

125

and cocked its head at the hunter.

"You are a Judas bird," he told it. The jay, still strangely silent, flew away.

Shadows were stretching long across the pond as the hunter headed back to the road. He skirted the edge of the pond again, and peered down. The swimming insects were gone. Only the spider was still there, motionless now.

More than a deer season was ending as the pale sun sank behind the pines.

(11/29/72)

DECEMBER

A TALE TOLD IN SNOW

Night fell lightly, seemingly suspended above the luminous snow. Soft shadows spilled from silent trees, stretched, then shrank slimmer, sharper to hide from the rising moon. A weasel peered from the hollow base of an ancient oak. Winter was awake. For the weasel is the synthesis of winter. Soft and sharp, beauty and beast, life and death.

Like a whisper of wind, the weasel moved toward the marsh, paired feet gently dimpling the drifts. Slender, sinuous, it slithered from sight like a white serpent, to pop back to the surface several feet away. It seemed frozen then, as if one with the snow, except for glittering eyes; twitching nose...

Nearby, where snow billowed over cattails, a rabbit shrank deeper into it form, sensing danger, round eyes unblinking in its canopied cavern. Aware now only of its drumming heart, of fleas astir in its downy underfur, and of the scent of death.

For the rabbit there never was a time to dare deep sleep. However, the weasel had slumbered soundly. Although no creature is more vibrantly alive in winter, the tiny killer could also sleep as though drugged, with no fear of being aroused. Even the fox, smelling the musky warning at the weasel's den, moved on to find less painful prey. So, even in sleep, the weasel never knows fear.

Boldly then, the weasel wove a trail across the marsh. Down to the scalloped banks of the creek, where inky currents chimed tinkling tunes against brittle borders of ice. There then, a warm scent seeped from the swamp. The weasel turned, bounded, sniffed. Sure now, yet haltingly, without haste, it advanced...

There was a moment when the rabbit might have run, even escaped the relentless wraith now poised nearby. But only a moment.

A fox perked its ears, an owl's eyes widened at the brief, muffled squall from the swamp.

The rabbit twitched as the weasel drank its fill. So fastidious that not a drop of blood stained its royal robe.

As the weasel abandoned the spot, the fox arrived. But the rabbit's carcass, if any remained, would not interest the weasel when it hungered again. It must kill anew.

Satiated, drowsy, the weasel crept back to its den. It curled there restlessly, nagged by the rabbit's fleas.

(12/02/67)

THE BALANCE

One of the meanest myths ever foisted on mankind is that there is -- or was -- a "balance of nature." Man alone, we would be led to believe, has knocked things askew and should now set them aright.

Well, I give up. Anybody who volunteers as a fulcrum in the nature balancing gambit should have a very pointed head -- in the absence of which a dunce cap might do.

It's the rabbits, mostly. Our country home has been in a state of siege. But for the fact that the house was built of brick, it might even now be tumbling down, victim of countless chiseling teeth.

We were kind to the rabbits, which lived in the marshlands bounding the woods behind our house. We'd take the dog down there and give them a bit of exercise, a little excitement now and then. They prospered and propagated as only healthy, excited rabbits can.

And then there was the brushpile. Anyone who has a woods and a fireplace inevitably must have a brush pile. Some people burn theirs. Ours was heaped higher and higher.

"The rabbits will like it," I explained to my wife when she scowled at the mountainous tangle growing within sight of the living room windows.

And they did.

The rabbits moved closer to the house. They cavorted across the lawn. By the time winter had set in they had become emboldened; fearless. We were surrounded. They danced before the headlights of my car as I drove up the long driveway after a week-long assignment upstate.

I noticed the red peach tree the next morning. I mean I noticed that it wasn't there. Only a sharp stub poked from the snowy turf. It would sprout again, I consoled myself. But moving on, I saw a young maple, girdled by ungrateful incisors. With rising panic, I hurried to a mountain ash, a honey locust, the hawthorn, the coffee tree. The trunks of all showed bands of white, barren of bark.

A flowering crab, a special present to my spouse, was doomed. The lilacs, the rose hedge, even an elm had been attacked.

"Doggone you doggone rabbits!" I wailed. "Sic 'em!" I shrieked, pushing the poor dog into the brushpile. The rabbits hid. No dumb bunnies, they.

Wire guards were quickly improvised for what remained of our yard trees, but a hurried investigation revealed that the rabbits were eating the entire woodlot. They were even devouring the brushpile, but I couldn't wait for them to eat themselves out of house and home. War was declared.

A wet snow fell overnight. It was an ideal time to put a torch to the brush. However, each time I kindled a roaring flame, snow capping the brush pile would melt and douse the blaze. I thought I heard a rabbit chuckle. Silently.

What I needed, I perceived, was a fox. One lives nearby, In fact, its den is within sight of our front door. But it shuns us and our rabbits. Not long ago our dog very nearly caught that fox by its silky red brush. The fox is still sulking about that.

Its tracks tell that the fox prefers to hunt mice in the neighbor's fields. Apparently, except for that burrow in our fence line, it wants nothing to do with us. So, we'll just have to make do with the dog.

There was hardly a rabbit on the place last year. And there were more foxes. That's how things really are, you see. The truth is that the wildlings bounce up and down on nature's scales like tots on a teeter-totter. Nature's balance is rarely static anywhere, anytime. It is more like a swinging pendulum. Or, sometimes, like a tower of children's blocks -- rising, teetering, toppling. Even this old earth wobbles on its axis.

Knowing that, I have readied the old bunny balancer for the next assault. It is a shotgun. Rabbits are legal targets. Good eating too.

But now I have a new worry. Down along the creek, trees are falling again. The old bachelor beaver must have returned, maybe this time with a family. If he builds a dam, neighbors upstream will complain, and we couldn't feed a whole family of beavers for very long.

But patience. Things change. Sometimes for the better.

If there is anything nature abhors more than a vacuum, it is the status quo.

(12/04/68)

132

HUSH OF WINTER

`The morning is hushed.

Muffled under fresh, billowed snow, the marsh sleeps.

Only a fox has preceded us down the path. Its tracks stitch a hem around a lacy tamarack; embroider a pattern amidst cedars flocked with fluffy snow and tinseled with ice. They skirt the creek, where a crooked snag is mirrored in dark water.

All summer a kingfisher kept vigil on that snag, a neatly uniformed sentinel reflected in a silver stream. It perched there when the buttercups bloomed and frogs sang. It kept its post while dogwoods flowered and when mints mixed their scent with the earthy odors of the swamp. It kept watch while tamaracks turned to golden steeples against the wine-hued oaks, the fiery maples and dappled hickories.

It was there, it seems, just yesterday.

But now fox tracks circle the squirrel's stump table, spread with fresh linen. They lead under glistening arches of briars, past places where pale, prickly shells of wild cucumber swing airily like frosted ornaments, through cattails wearing cottony caps.

And all is still.

There were dawns, not long ago, when there were concerts of birdsong here; when the creek rippled with the wakes of wood ducks; when the kingfisher perched patiently on the snag.

This morning, this moment, we walk the path alone. Only a fox has arrived before us.

Only a fox...and winter.

(12/17/64)

133

WOODPILE MUSINGS

Behind the barn is a big pile of wood which I whittle away at during my leisure. There are few things more invigorating than making firewood on a cold day. Swinging an axe makes blood sing in your veins. But there's more to it than that. Chopping wood gives a man time and room to meditate.

The fates provided bountifully for the fireplace this winter. Early last summer, a windstorm toppled two big oaks and snapped some hickories in our woods. And there's also much dead elm these days if you're willing to work for it.

Most of the oak and hickory was cut and split earlier, but the elm was left until cold crept deep into its grain, making the tough wood a bit more brittle. Few things in nature are so resistant to a man's labors. The fibrous sapwood is unyielding. It grasps the splitting wedge with a vise-like grip, so you search for faults which betray routes which the wedge might follow. Then, slab by slab, shaggy shards are laid upon the ground.

I think about the elms which stood so strong when snow and ice snapped the tops from pines. I think of those I've seen thrive after being seared and scarred by fire. I remember those which withstood a tornado that shattered oaks and snapped hemlocks like straws. The elms were bent, twisted, sometimes uprooted, but they would not yield a branch. Most survived.

And then along came a tiny fungus, riding on a bit of a beetle, and the elm trees died. That is a profound thing to think about.

I think too, about how much faster the winter's wood might have been laid up with the help of a power saw. But they shriek and stink and there is no pleasure in them. I like to smell the chips showering from the axe blade. I like the chant sung by a crosscut saw and the glad ring of the wedge when at last the wood has yielded.

I think then about our growing slavery to the internal combustion engine; about ruts gouged into roadless areas; about tracks left by snarling scooters as they spin and churn up mountainsides; about snowmobiles which howl and fume across once-silent lakes and through pine-scented woods.

I recall my annoyance at the scream of chain saws in the heart of the wilderness canoe area in the Superior National Forest -- and the federal rangers' answer that they would just put mufflers on them. I remembered, in that same area, hearing the whine of an outboard motor which had been carried over many portages by hired guides. And I wondered how many moose, mink and otters their clients never saw.

I think that, in our haste, we often speed by -- even overrun --that which we seek. I think that, unless we draw lines beyond which machines may not pass, man himself will be ground through the gears.

And, as the wedge rings in the clear air, I think of how my wife loves to sit by a flickering fire; how the children will roast marshmallows over the coals. And how many kinds of warmth -- and even truth -- can be hewn from a pile of wood.

(12/22/64)

WINTER MARSH

The frozen marsh seems forlorn and still, containing only cold ashes of summers' warmth. But look closer. It is a banked fire. Life is held snugly in the warm embrace of its grasses and the soft bosom of its mud.

Turtles stir deeper into the ooze where swamp deepens into pond. There too, minnows are suspended in the dark water. They appear motionless, but tiny currents from their pulsing gills stir leaves still adrift under the ice.

Nearby, a cottontail rabbit creeps cautiously from its bed in the marsh grass. New snow has blurred the tracks of the fox which meandered near during the night, but the rabbit had found shelter and warmth under an arch of matted stems. And safety, for another night, from the fox, the owl, and the sharp wind.

Now a pheasant peeks out from under the thatched roof of its roost. It stalks stiffly away, through the red dogwoods, printing a row of crooked crosses in the snow.

A cardinal whistles, one small, thin note. As if on signal, chickadees appear, so suddenly that they seem to have popped from empty milkweed pods. Feathers fluffed against the cold, they look like rotund caricatures of their summer selves.

A deer is bedded under the tamaracks nearby. It sleeps in a robe of hollow hairs as warm as the chickadee's down. But only in such sheltered spots as these will such insulation suffice when blizzards blow.

The Arctic wind is a scythe, colder and sharper than steel. But its edge is dulled; its blade buried by fragile stems and brittle, broken leaves. And that is a marsh, when winter comes.

(12/23/63)

ON WINTER NIGHTS

Winter has crept softly into our woods by night. Deceptively quiet, seemingly unseen. Yet, it has not escaped notice.

The wind may caress and lie, but there is cold truth in the sky. Knowing, in a way past understanding, the wild ones cling closer when winter comes.

The nuthatch knows nothing of winter solstices, but it somehow reads the sundial of the seasons. When noonday shadows stretch far toward the north, it will not stray far from the security of seeds and suet in our yard.

The raccoon recognizes no figures in the stars, but it rarely roams far from its den on nights when Orion and his hounds are hunting across the heavens.

Things draw closer on winter nights. Crows huddle in the pines. Chickadees congregate in cedars. Squirrels cuddle in hollow oaks. Deer gather. Coyotes chorus. There is comfort in company.

Indeed, all creation comes close after winter sunsets. Stars draw nearer, casting a jeweled net across the deep darkness, and we can see the Milky Way, that giant, glittering pinwheel whirling us through space, lighting the trail across our galaxy.

There are nights too, when the aurora streams from the Arctic sky, flickering, flashing, shining, shifting. Its form and hues are as indescribable as its sighs.

A familiar trail through the woods seems somehow strange as I stroll through the cold darkness. There is the moon, shining through the black lace of tamarack boughs. It casts shadows of cattails, marching like soldiers along the frozen fringes of the creek.

Lights of neighbors' houses, hidden in summer, now wink through leafless trees. There is the scent of wood smoke from distant chimneys. The creek signs a soft carol to its stones.

Oh silent night...

Somewhere a dog barks. A door slams. A truck snorts along a far-off highway, The spell is broken.

Time then, to carry another armload of wood to the house, and watch with loved ones as warm colors skip across the hearth.

Things gather close on winter nights.

(12/25/67)

THE SOLSTICE

The woods seem asleep. Night...and winter...have fallen softly. The meadow lies under a quilt of snow. Chipmunk and acorn are dormant in the earth. Buntings roost snugly in the cedars.

Nature seems at rest. Squirrels snoozing in cozy dens. Cocoons cradling caterpillars. Sumacs snuggled in fur fine as velvet.

But the brook is awake. It chuckles through a rapids, pausing in a pool to mirror the sky, winking back at the stars, the constellations of winter.

Orion the Hunter stalks across the heavens these nights, shining sword buckled to glittering belt. The dog stars, Sirius and Procyon travel with him. Lepus the Hare and Ursus the Bear ever keep their distance.

Smaller dramas will be played out in the woods this night. A rabbit, soundless as its moon shadow, creeps from its place in the tamaracks. Yet quieter, an owl follows on hushed wings. A weasel slithers under the snow in silent search of mice. A fox slinks toward a pheasant's roost in the marsh.

Pain of death or pang of hunger? For prey and predator, that question must be answered each night as the hunter and his hounds trek across the sky. Each night the answer is more critical to the survivors below.

Still there is peace where the brook meanders through the marsh. It murmurs lullabies to frogs asleep in the mud. It slowly swirls through eddies where black ducks doze. It burbles under frosted ferns where a doe stops to sip. It is a long trail the doe must travel, growing heavy with fawn, before the frogs will answer the brook in song.

Until then there may be nights when green fires flicker in the sky; when icy barriers try to stay the brook's journey to the sea. Nights when solid sap explodes from trees; when even Orion's progress seems halted in a frozen sky.

Yet, there is the promise that such things will not last. Tomorrow the sun will rise a bit earlier and linger moments longer. Slowly, slowly its slanting beams will begin to bore through winter's icy armor.

The December solstice has just arrived and Orion's hunt is far from over. Still, the longest night is also the eve of lengthening days. The awakening has begun.

(12/26/66)

ON A BALMY DAY

Sarona, Wis. -- There was this day when winter turned away; when the morning wind seemed wet and warm like a puppy's kiss and the snow settled with soft sighs.

There was this place along a winding forest road where a frozen lake beckoned to see what was beyond. And these are the things I found:

In the wooded hills, gray squirrels peered from the tops of den trees. Fat. Still feasting on a huge harvest of nuts. Their tracks and burrowings were everywhere.

Deer too. Still moving freely as they followed trails now hidden, yet remembered beneath the sticky snow. The trails led far from the overbrowsed yards where deer are imprisoned when winter works its worst. Each day of escape means more life to meet the spring.

On a hillside, I walked amid old pine stumps, ragged remnants of the giants which once dominated this land. Charred by fearsome fires, they still jut starkly from the drifts. They are surrounded now by hardwoods, except for a few scattered survivors of their kind, found by the sun before forest succession darkened the cutover.

From the hollow of such a stump, a tiny saw-whet owl fluttered softly to a nearby branch and watched in wide-eyed wonderment at my intrusion. Time forgotten, I had traveled far from the trails of men. The snow began to stiffen. The wind was sharpening. Winter had not gone far, or for long.

With a few curls of birch bark and some shards shattered from a stump, I soon had a fire jousting with the wind. My knapsack yielded a simple lunch. It was time to turn back. But not before climbing another ridge and rounding a hidden pond.

There, telltale stains and litter on the snow prompted an upward look. Clinging to a swaying branch, a porcupine stolidly returned my gaze. It appeared to be content, even cozy on its breezy perch. I knew its secret: Beneath its bristling quills a porcupine wears a coat of fur.

There too, was a little red squirrel scurrying up a shaggy pine, and hairy woodpecker inspecting the bark of a bitternut hickory.

A bit farther on, I paused to study coyote tracks, printed during the morning thaw. The depressions had become pitfalls for snowfleas, which now darkened the tracks against the snow. And then there was a place where an otter had bounded and bellyflopped across the snow to go from pond to pond. And a weasel's tracks, stitched daintily from stump to stump. And oval holes chiseled into a long dead snag by a pileated woodpecker.

The wind died as day waned. The woods were hushed. Even chickadees were quiet. For a time, the loudest sound was the rasping of a raven's wings, flapping darkly across the still, gray sky.

Then, still some distance from where I'd left the truck, I heard snowmobiles approaching. Closer. Louder.

They careened by, eight of them. Their riders waved happily as they crossed the pond and rocketed over the ridge. Slowly then, the silence returned.

My musings were still on my backtrail as, pace quickening, I headed for the road.

Those snowmobilers had already traveled far, much farther than roaming feet had carried me this day.

And I wondered what they had seen.

(12/28/74)

SNOW WRITINGS

The swamp beckoned as the old dog and I trekked down the hill on our morning hike. Tattered cattails waved a welcome in the wintry wind. Ice had armored the marsh during the frigid night, so the trail to the tamaracks was open to us once more.

The dog romped ahead, glad to have fresh territory to explore. I followed, just as curious, for a swamp has many secrets well hidden in summer.

A dusting of snow provided a ledger for taking inventory as we crackled through the brittle, brown reeds. Mouse tracks stitched a trail from one grassy hummock to another. A fox had stopped to sniff, then meandered on, certain that there was bigger game not far ahead.

I marveled that the fox had been there so soon. It too, must have been watching, waiting for the freeze-up. I wondered how many generations of foxes had done so. For 20 years I have hiked through that frozen hollow almost every winter day. And always, the foxes have been there first.

I tracked this one, reading its foxy thoughts. It knew that the cottontails had moved into the tamaracks too.

Although often beautiful, and always valuable, wetlands are not inviting places in summer. They buzz with biting insects and try to entrap trespassers in rank-smelling ooze. Not only humans, but other terrestrial mammals shun them then.

And among wetlands, swamps have especially bad reputations as hostile places. But what is a swamp, anyway?

Swamp, marsh and bog all have nearly identical definitions in my dictionary: "A lowland saturated with water," or "wet, spongy ground," seems to cover them all.

But while those kinds of wetlands may meet and merge, they do differ, I distinguish them this way:

A bog is a very old lake, mostly covered with a floating mat of vegetation. The water is dark, and so acid that bog plants can scarcely drink it. They live in a wet desert, and have made many adaptations to survive.

A marsh is an area dominated by rushes, reeds and cattails. Usually there is a flow of water, however imperceptible. The water is sweeter than in a bog.

And a swamp? It's a wetland distinguished by trees. We speak of cypress swamps, cedar swamps, spruce swamps.

Ours then, is a tamarack swamp, encircled by a marsh.

From spring to winter, the area is negotiable only in hip boots, and then with great difficulty. After freeze-up though, access is easy. Rabbits retreat to the swamp. Birds hide there from Arctic winds. Deer sometimes take refuge in the cattails.

And every day there are new stories written in the snow.

Summer's reminders were everywhere as we crossed the marsh this first morning after freeze-up. Nightshade berries still glowed like rubies. The ice encircled clumps of still-green ferns. A redwing's nest still clung to broken reeds.

Marsh milkweeds, silken seeds long since tossed to the winds, rattled their empty husks as we brushed by. In the bare, brown stalks of goldenrods, clustered on little islands, were swellings where gall flies had laid their eggs. I snapped off some of the bulging stems and stuffed them in a pocket. The tiny grubs inside would make good panfish baits, and ice fishing time was nigh.

As we approached the border of alder, holly and dogwood which flanks the swamp, a cardinal fluttered away, a flash of fire amid frosty branches. And ahead, under the trees, gray wraiths of rabbits drifted silently away.

Rabbits have been abundant this fall, but now they will be fewer each day until spring. The dog stopped to sniff at a patch of stained, fur-strewn snow. The fox had dined.

However, the fox's life will no be so easy when the rabbits are fewer and warier. Times may be lean when little foxes arrive in the den in the still-frozen earth next spring.

Leaving the tamaracks, we walked the edge of a trail of spring water which seeps down to the creek. Spotted salamanders slumber there in the mud, oblivious to winter travails of predator and prey. Frogs dream there of songs they'll sing in spring. And turtles sleep, all tucked in, as only turtles can.

Black ducks, the wariest of the wild, were dabbling in the creek again, now that hunting season was past. They exploded into flight as we rounded the bend. But it was time for them to make their morning move anyway; time to join the geese now clamoring overhead, bound for a field of corn stubble a mile away.

Nearing the house, I paused at the woodpile, measuring it in my mind, picturing how much it would diminish in a week, a month, a season. I ought to spend more time making wood, I concluded, and less time poking around in swamps.

Behind us, crows were sailing into the tamaracks, sharp eyes studying the snow, below, muttering amongst themselves, complaining that the fox had left nothing for them.

It was all part of an old pattern, ever repeated. Yet every day is new. And winter has just begun.

(12/28/84)

JANUARY

KEEPING WARM

If we're so smart, why can't we cope with winter as well as many dumb animals do?

That question cut as keenly as the wind as I shoveled through the driveway drifts this morning, dug out the mailbox and returned to the house with another armload of oak.

Not far from the woodpile a woodchuck sleeps. Freshly excavated earth revealed the whereabouts of its new burrow as winter neared. Snug under the snow, thermostat turned down to conserve energy, the woodchuck now snoozes blissfully, dreaming of sunny summer days and rows of rutabagas.

On the wooded hill behind the house is a hollow tree with an entrance worn smooth by chipmunk traffic. The hole leads to a tunnel beneath the roots, then to bedrooms, pantries filled with nuts and seeds; even a latrine. Hyperactive all summer, chipmunks can't quite slow down to the woodchuck's pace when winter comes. But they sleep a lot, and know better than to poke their noses outside until half past April.

In a bigger tree down near the creek, squirrels cuddle. When weather moderates they'll bound to the backyard feeder again, but they've added not a track to the snow since the thermometer slipped below zero.

Nor has the fox visited our woods and marsh on recent nights, When most other wildlife is lying low beneath the snow, the predator takes a cue from its prey. The fox somehow understands that, while winter is working its worst, hunting can consume more calories than could be caught. So, curled in den or hollow, the fox warms its nose with its tail. And waits.

Rabbits are huddling in snow-roofed brushpiles, nibbling bark from the leftovers of my labors with ax and saw. Bigger parts of the trees were split and stacked for fuel, but I suspect that the rabbits make more efficient use of their share than I do of mine.

Even birds are scarce at the feeders when the wind chill factor is hovering around 40 below. It is better to fluff one's feathers and stay in the hushed shelter of the cedars than to be buffeted by Arctic blasts while getting a few seeds or bits of suet.

But of course, not all wildlife hides from winter. For example, the mallards which winter on our creek. The currents there may be briefly stilled by ice during winter's bitterest periods. Yet, soon after the mercury rises above zero, the ducks are dabbling there again.

If you've ever plucked the full winter plumage from a duck or goose, you won't wonder why they don't shiver. A quilt of fluffy down lies beneath those waterproof, windproof feathers, and a special circulatory arrangement keeps the exposed legs and feet from freezing.

Further, if the ducks didn't like it, they could just take the next flight south. And with no winter storm tie-ups at the airport. So are we really so superior?

I recall an anthropology class wherein a smug professor assured us that man is the most successful animal because he has been the most adaptable. Big brains, opposable thumbs and the ability to get around on our hind legs have moved us into everything from thatched huts and igloos to condominiums.

But other creatures survive, and even thrive, with none of those.

Blowing on my stinging fingers this morning, I was more convinced than ever that we will never adapt to these latitudes as well as the lowly frog, bedded beneath the creek until another spring.

(01/03/79)

THE TRAFFIC CHECK

Snowdrifts were heaped high overnight in our woods and marsh. They lay gently on the iron earth; the flinty ice.

Rosy as a woodchopper's cheeks, the sun peeked through the tamaracks. The radio reported a temperature near zero in the city, and already a man in a helicopter was describing a snarl of traffic in the fresh snow below.

It seemed like a good time to take a traffic check along the creek.

A small mystery was solved by the first tracks I found. Dainty etchings in the snow, they led to and from a small burrow near the base of an oak. Until early autumn, yellowjackets were quartered in that little den. Then, one cool night a skunk ambled by, stopped to sniff, and then to dig. It feasted on the sleepy insects and left the burrow vacant, surrounded by tatters of the hornets' nest.

But on a frigid day before the snow, I noted a rim of frost glistening around the mouth of the burrow. Some small creature breathed below. I had guessed a chipmunk, but the snow told that it was a whitefooted mouse.

The mouse probably was displaced recently when a nearby, windfelled oak was cut up for firewood. The hollow trunk had housed a mouse nest. The burrow may be a poor substitute, but it will keep its new occupant secure -- so long as the earth remains frozen, to foil the predators' paws.

Farther along, tracks told where two rabbits had crept from the marsh and bounded across the frozen creek while the snow still drifted down.

Although blurred, the prints plainly showed how each had sprinted across the clearing before an owl could swoop.

A third cottontail track, smaller, angled through the cattails. It revealed that there was still a least one survivor from an uncommonly late litter. I will likely be an early casualty, for even mature rabbits face awesome odds.

Researchers once tagged 226 wild cottontails in southern Michigan, and reported only two still living after two years. In Iowa, a biologist started with a September census of 284 rabbits on 186 acres, and found only 41 surviving on Jan. 1. Only 10 had been taken by human hunters. And winter's worst was still to come.

There now, a red fox had meandered along the creek, turning into the rushes, emerging again still hungry. The fox had headed up the hill and paused where a woodchuck sleeps deep beneath the cedars. It savored scent in the wind wafting past our chicken coop; then sensed danger in the doghouse adjacent to the coop. The fox turned again and trotted on. Hungry still.

It was already an old story in an old book when Henry Thoreau read from it in January, 1841:

"Here was one expression of the divine mind this morning," wrote Thoreau, after following the winding path of a fox across Walden pond.

A weasel had circled an old oak snag on the hillside. I could picture it, moving in fluid bounds, feet placed primly in pairs. Head high, sniffing, peering myopically into the white night.

Two pheasants had strode across the marsh. My dog followed their tracks into the tamaracks. Two hens flushed on muffled wings.

But the inventory could not be completed. It was too cold. There were no muskrat tracks around the domed house in the marsh. The raccoons had napped through another night. Skunks and chipmunks slumbered. Even the 'possum had taken refuge somewhere. It's odd, splayed tracks and the sinuous trail of its tail were nowhere to be seen.

Neither had the old bachelor beaver left any fresh signs in our much-gnawed popple patch. I think he has moved to a new abode in the creek bank, well downstream.

The sun was dazzling as I turned back. Stark shadows printed a pattern where a squirrel had ventured to its cache beneath a hickory. It had apparently wasted no time in returning to its snug den. I understood why.

Boots squeaking, ears stinging, I hurried toward the house. Even the dog seemed anxious to reach the warmth behind the door.

Back inside, sipping coffee, I gazed through the windows. The snow looked like a layer of wool. Yes, a blanket. There is more truth than triteness in that description. During winter's worst, temperatures have been found to be as much as 60 degrees warmer under seven inches of fluffy snow. A grouse knows that. So does a mouse.

The radio announcer was repeating warnings about the weather:

"The first full-scale plowing and salting operations of the year are under way on city streets," he said.

And it struck me that, of all the tracks made in the snow, the strangest by far are made by man.

(01/04/68)

A WINTER DAWN

Dawn is drawing a pale yellow line along the brink of the horizon, a cold brass rail at the edge of the frozen earth. Sounds confirm that the temperature is below zero. There is the brittle crunch of snow as the dog an I start down the path; the papery crackling of my quilted jacket as I pull a knit cap over my ears.

Winter. Brrrr. Bah!

But it is like taking that first shivery plunge into a lake on a summer day. By the time we reach the woods the air feels more bracing than chilling. Our pace quickens.

Chips is circling a brushpile, taking the canine equivalent of a cottontail count. The spaniel's nose tells him that the rabbit population is dwindling steadily, as it has since late autumn. We have found the trails's end for a score of them -- tufts of fur on the stained snow.

Each night the hollow hootings of owls are heard. Tracks of a questing fox are printed in each new snow. And yet rabbits continue to appear. It is as if the brushpile were a magician's hat. However, after years of marveling at the trick, one concludes that the magic is not in the hat, but in the rabbit.

Other wonders are nearby. Pockmarks in the crusted snow, surrounded by shards of shell, tell how unerringly a squirrel retrieves its treasures.

Now day yawns. Its first deep breath rattles through cattails in the marsh. On a wooded hill, a few more stubborn oak leaves lose their grips and flutter down. They scuttle across the glazed snow, as if looking for places to hide.

Where the trail nears the creek, we find that a fox has killed again. There, where the wind has not swept a dusting of snow from the glaze, tracks tell that a fox has carried something from the dogwoods, something so large that it dragged. Following, we find a tuft of fur to confirm that it was a cottontail. The tracks lead through the frozen marsh and turn to follow the creek. There, where springfed currents steam, the fox sat on its haunches, pausing to rest.

It seems curious that the fox has carried its prey so far before feeding. There are no young to care for now. Perhaps its belly was already full of mice and voles, abundant this winter. Maybe the fox had simply leaped at opportunity when it met the rabbit, and was taking it to a more secure cache for future use.

Deep in the tamaracks the answer is revealed. The tracks of another fox are met. Evidence of romping is seen in the snow. The rabbit devoured, the couple left together.

It seems a bit soon, this frigid morning, for the courtship of foxes to begin. But then, the foxes would be the better judges of that. Still, one fact bemuses: It was the smaller fox, almost certainly the vixen, which brought the rabbit to the nuptial banquet.

Crows, uncommonly quiet, ride the rising wind as a brassy sun appears. Almost nothing escapes their eyes. Not the shreds of skin and fragments of bone where the foxes dined. Not kernels of corn exposed where deer have pawed in a stubble field. Not the horned owl in a tall cedar, sleeping with one eye open.

Owl discovered, the crows rally, hurling raucous insults. The owl looks like a dignified jurist who has myopically misplaced his gavel. Unable to restore order, the owl retreats, looking grumpy and rumpled.

Mallard ducks have spent the night in the steamy currents of the creek. To one observing them all winter, it seems evident that many of them are paired. Unlike geese, which mate for life, ducks supposedly pair only for a season. I suspect that the ducks on our creek think differently.

The climbing sun gives an illusion of warmth, but numbing toes are not so easily deceived. It is time to head back to the house. As we climb back up the hill, two clear, descending notes are heard. Pausing, we hear them reassuringly repeated. It is a call that will be heard oftener as midday shadows shorten. It is a chickadee making a cheering prediction; a promise.

But then, the foxes have already assured us that spring is on the way.

(01/08/81)

HIDING FROM THE COLD

A chickadee, puffed to twice its normal size, watched from the lee side of the bird feeder as the dog and I left the house.

Usually the most cheerful of birds, the chickadee clung disconsolately to its wind-buffeted perch as we passed. I wondered where the others were.

Of the many birds that come to our offerings of sunflower seeds, chickadees are the ones which remain visible during winter's cruelest weather. When the wind chill is in double digits below zero, cardinals, nuthatches, purple finches, goldfinches, grosbeaks, juncos, and even the indomitable jays go into hiding.

Maybe most of them are simply huddled in the sheltered cedars just down the hill. Even so, it's unlikely that all have survived. For three days and nights now, the wind has sliced through the woods like a scythe.

Birds that dwell in hollows are least vulnerable to such cutting cold. Woodpeckers are therefor still flying regular sorties to the suet sack. A downy woodpecker has modified a bluebird house for its winter quarters. The hairy and redheaded woodpeckers have homes in hollow trees.

Other species, including chickadees, nuthatches and jays, also will hide in hollows. However, there are never enough dens for all. Owls, raccoons and squirrels claim the biggest and best. The pecking order continues from there. Then, like a hungry wolf, winter finds the outcasts, the weak.

But survival is the rule, even in the snarling, biting, gnawing cold a Wisconsin winter can bring. Best-adapted are hibernators, such as the woodchuck, which is oblivious to winter scenes above its burrow. Skunks sleep soundly too. The chipmunk stirs, but stays in snug chambers -- complete with pantry and latrine.

Some species suffer because they have not really adapted to the rigors of these latitudes. The pheasant, a transplant from milder climes, is a frequent victim of severe winters. Wisconsin also is the northern frontier for some native species, such as the opossum and bobwhite quail. Whole coveys of quail may perish in extended subzero weather. And the opossum, not a denning animal, can lose its tail and ears, if not its life, to winter's teeth.

Rabbits have no tails to worry about, but it seems that their ample ears would be vulnerable to frostbite. Not so. Cottontails and snowshoe hares keep warm by huddling in "forms" -- sheltered hollows in the snow. Their soft, fragile-seeming fur is so warm for its weight that rabbit-skin blankets were much favored by the native Americans.

Swamps offer protection from the wind and are hideouts for much wildlife, including deer. So sheltered, a well-fed whitetail, wrapped in its coat of hollow hairs, is able to withstand almost any degree of cold. It is deep snow, not cold, which is deadliest to deer. It can trap them in overbrowsed winter yards and it can make them easy prey.

Bears are luckier. The colder it gets, the sounder they sleep. Although not a true hibernator, a bear spends most of the winter in a deep snooze. Female bears expecting to give birth in midwinter usually prepare a snug den. On the other hand, a big old male may just back into a fallen tree, scratch a heap of leaves around him and doze through winter's snows. Thick fur and a layer of fat are the bears barriers against the cold.

The chickadee was still huddled alone at the feeder as we returned to the house. It was a reminder that winter tests, and that some will fail.

Yet, most -- large and small, furred and feathered, predator and prey -- will endure these times of trial.

And perhaps like us, they all have dreams of spring.

(01/13/83)

A WINTER WINDOW

Winter's fangs are flashing at the window, icicles gleaming from the eaves. Beneath and beyond, the north wind is gnawing swirls and scallops in the crusting snow. Their shadows etch sharp patterns as the sun creeps into a pale blue sky.

This late January morning would be a fine time to listen to the squeaky whispers of snowshoes in dry snow, to find the stopping place of those black ducks seen at dusk, to learn where the urgings of the fox have led him overnight. However, I confess a preference some mornings for remaining at my window in the woods, warmed by the fire, watching shadows of chimney smoke while squinting at the dazzling view outside. The window frames some of my favorite scenes in every season, but on such frigid days its vantage point is particularly appealing.

Far from being a simple study in black and white, winter is a parade of colorful happenings in the country. Now the oaks look starkly dead, their dark trunks patched with snow; shrouded limbs still clutched by brittle leaves which rattle in the wind, but along the creek there is already a russet glow in the redosier's bark, and a yellow gleam appearing in the willows.

Then too, there is the way snow glows blue in the moonlight, turns subtly pink at dawn; then sparkles with evanescent rainbows as the wind swirls it toward the sun. And the way cardinals perch in a winter-tinseled cedar, putting the most elaborately ornamented Christmas tree to shame.

Juncos, hooded capes drawn snugly over their snowy vests, are the first to flutter down to the feeder these days. Perhaps they arise early to avoid the bullying bluejays. The juncos seem to have accepted a lone tree sparrow as a winter companion. He regularly arrives and leaves with the little flock. The cardinals and purple finches arrive next, along with an increasing variety of others.

More species are attracted to the feeder as winter progresses, a sign that food is becoming scarcer in the wilds behind the house. Berries are gone. Many seeds are buried beneath the snow. Insects and their eggs have been gleaned from tree bark. So now the feeder brings hairy and downy woodpeckers and even a flicker. A redheaded woodpecker still disdains a handout, but he shouldn't be proud of it. I know his secret. He is thriving on acorns cached by the nuthatches. However, the victims of such thievery continue to carry seeds from the feeder to tuck them under shaggy hickory bark, so perhaps the redhead is enjoying our provisions after all.

Crows perch nearby, calling, eyeing the seeds and suet, yet too wary to yield to the temptation. Resourceful birds, crows can find provender in the worst of times, but such easy pickings are hard to pass up.

The cheerful chickadees seem to keep no regular schedule. Like wind-tossed thistledown, they ride the gusts, tumbling around the feeder like acrobatic clowns. What a contrast with the woodchuck who sleeps under the wooded slope beyond the feeder. Even in sleep, the chickadees' heart beats 500 times per minute; in flight perhaps twice as often. And in the same span of time, life pulses but seven times in the woodchuck.

Spring may seem distant indeed when the mercury is shivering at the bottom of the thermometer and last summer's oriole nest is a basket of snow, swaying from a frosty limb. Nonetheless, the mating moon has risen for horned owls.

No cozy hollow will shelter the owls' eggs. Usually the nest is an exposed structure which was originally built by a redtailed hawk or a squirrel. The owlets often must endure some of winter's worst. No wonder then, that they look so fierce, even while still covered with down.

The fox too, feels new yearnings. He may keep to his den for days when winter is most wrathful, but as the days lengthen he roves farther, stopping to sleep on sunny slopes, warming his nose with his fine tail. Before long now, fox tracks will be found in pairs.

Squirrels are seeking company too. A pair scampers among the trees down near the creek bank. One pauses to unerringly dig an acorn from a cache safe from woodpeckers. Its tail twitches nervously while its head is buried in the snow, for such blind exposure can be fatal.

From my window I can also see the marsh where muskrats are snug in domed houses, and a slope where tiny snapping turtles sleep, fully formed but still encased in leathery shells. I know, for my exploring shovel revealed them there, even as winter was beginning to turn the earth to iron.

Marvelous, when you ponder them, the adaptations which various forms of life have made to winter.

But it is plain to see, from my side of a frosty window, that man has been the most adaptable of all.

(01/23/70)

HARD WINTER

How quiet is the cold as another dawn approaches.

So still that snow squeaks loudly underfoot. So silent that the owl's hushed wings are as a rush of wind through the trees.

How brittle the black shadows, shattering into sharp shards when moonbeams strike. The scene seems etched by cold. The air stings like acid on nose and cheeks.

A hostile world awaits as my spaniel sidekick and I begin a walk before dawn. If a prober from another planet now visited our swamp, I imagine it would discover this Earth to be uninhabitable.

Unless, of course, it had sensors as sophisticated as a springer spaniel's nose.

Chips knows that a rabbit has been hiding in a certain brushpile for days. He knows that two pheasants -- one a longtailed, loudmouthed rooster, the other a demure hen -- are snug in a snowcapped hideout under the arched reeds. He knows of mice and mourning doves, and the wanderings of weasels.

At his urgings then, I follow, masked and mittened, to learn what has survived another Arctic night.

The winter has not been kind to wildlife and the worst cruelty may yet come. Stabbing cold already has bled the strength of animals that don't retreat into winter sleep. But even the dens of many hibernators may be chilled by the penetrating cold.

Effects of such stress is hard to measure, but this much is certain: It takes far more fuel to keep life's fire lit in subzero weather. However, energy expended to obtain a meal may be greater than the gain.

Wildlife instinctively knows this. That is why there have been no fresh fox tracks on recent nights. The fox is aware that it is wiser to curl its tail around its nose, bank the fire and endure an empty stomach. Meanwhile, the rabbit keeps to its brushpile, gnawing bark from the branches therein, warm enough anywhere the wind cannot ruffle its downy fur.

Raccoons too, are keeping to their dens. Not one track has been seen along the creek since late November. And squirrels stray from shelter only as long and far as necessary to unearth a meal of acorns.

The squirrel hasn't far to dig, but shallow snow depths are a mixed blessing. Even in the north woods, deer can range widely to feed, but the ruffed grouse suffers for lack of deep, fluffy drifts it needs for roosting on frigid nights.

Thinly insulated, the lakes and marshes have been freezing ever deeper. Muskrats and beavers have become vulnerable, forced to search elsewhere for food and water.

But even in such times, there are signs that not all is despair. The fox, when it resumes its roaming, will start seeking a mate. Even now, horned owls are readying their nests.

And just this morning, just at dawn, two sweet, muted notes were heard from the tamaracks. Softly, as if the bird were practicing under its breath, they sounded again as the sun inched into a frosty sky.

That call melted the icy silence and warmed the heart as we climbed the hill to the house. It had reminded us that long nights are shortening; that even the longest winters must surely end.

For down in the frozen swamp, a chickadee had sung of spring.

(01/20/77)

THE RESPITE

The resonant call of a hen mallard heralded the good news as the spaniel and I began our early morning trek. Winter had relented, freeing the spring-fed creek from the icy grip which had held it for more than two weeks. Sensing that, the ducks had returned, winging unerringly through dense fog to splash down at the bend behind our house.

The woods seemed strange. The trees were out-of-focus sketches in the luminous mist. Damp air caressed cheeks accustomed to clawing cold. It would not last, of course, but it was respite for the wild ones. I thought about a rabbit met the morning before. The encounter had changed my perspective on winter woes.

Crouched at the edge of the woods, the cottontail had watched with quiet desperation as I approached on snowshoes. My dog, weary from wallowing through drifts, remained obediently at heel as I mushed to within 10 feet of the rabbit. When it finally moved, it was to flounder only a few feet through the deep, fluffy snow. It seemed uninjured. Just exhausted; resigned.

Hiking on, I looked back to see the rabbit hop into my tracks, which were tamped deeply enough to offer some shelter from the cutting wind. I wondered why it had abandoned the relative safety of a big brushpile nearby. Maybe rabbits suffer from "cabin fever" too.

Such neurotic rabbits are doubtless appreciated by the red-tailed hawk who perches in our woods for hours, eyes agleam with hunger. And there are other perils. Nightly now, hollow hootings tell that horned owls are pairing. There will be more hungry beaks in our woods before

166

winter is gone.

So, although I reject the adage that misery loves company, empathy for the rabbit did make my own problems shrink.

Our long, winding driveway has become a deep, narrow trench through the snow, almost impossible to plow. The woodpile is shrinking alarmingly, almost disappearing under the advancing drifts. Snow is burdening the roof and burying the fences. The truck is balking.

But all of those seem mere inconveniences compared to the rabbit's struggles this harsh winter.

Of course, I know better than to wax sentimental about rabbits. As a species, they are experts in survival, routinely rebounding from hardship to produce surpluses which threaten our garden.

Mindful of all that, I trekked down the trail today with my pockets full of corn. There were still some kernels left to welcome the ducks when I reached the creek.

(01/24/79)

EARLY BIRDS

Crows are first to break the quiet of wintry dawns. Flapping across a leaden sky, they call greetings to the first glimmer of light as the spaniel and I begin our morning trek.

They are eastbound usually, as if hurrying to meet another day. Two here, three there, sharp eyes searching for a stain in the snow, a patch of fur along the road. Long winter nights gnaw at life, and hunger does not sleep.

The bleakest day brings discoveries to those of us, airborne or earthbound, who have appetite for the quest.

There was this morning when there was a softness to the dawn. Fresh, fluffy snow had fallen and the wind was but a whisper in the trees. The creek, recently stilled by subzero nights, once more rippled between snowy borders. It gleamed like silver in the early light; then glowed like molten brass as the sun neared the horizon.

A pair of mallards watched warily as we drew near; then relaxed, dabbling and chuckling, as we turned back to toward the marsh. Periodic absences of open water are an inconvenience to the hardy ducks, but they never seem discomfited by the cold. The drake's finery of emerald green, chestnut brown, natty gray and white is no warmer than the hen's tan coat. Both are weatherproof coverings for luxurious layers of down.

Three pairs of mallards and as many black ducks are regular winter callers to the springfield creek. Authorities say that pairings don't occur until spring migration, but it must be more than coincidence that our winter ducks are usually seen as couples.

A deer had passed through the woods before the snow stopped. A big buck, I surmised from the size of the bounding tracks. Deer tracks are not often seen around our place in winter. That one apparently knew where he was going. He had not hesitated in our woods.

A pheasant's tracks, blurred by new snow, meandered into the marsh. In the woods, tiny prints of mouse feet stitched trails from tree to tree. There was a place where a rabbit had poked out of the tamarack swamp and ducked back into the snowy tangle as we approached. The dog sniffed the fresh scent and bounded in tail-wagging pursuit. It is an old game for both of them, --and for the rabbit, a tame pastime compared to nightly visits of fox and owl.

Some mornings there is something new. There may be tracks of a wandering weasel, or prints of a raccoon, beckoned from its den by a thawing night. But one recent morning I was perplexed by a strange track which paralleled the trail. It had apparently been made by a small, bounding beast which dragged its tail. I puzzled over it for several strides before the truth dawned: My wife had used her new walking stick, a Christmas present, while walking the dog the previous afternoon.

But not every visitor leaves prints in the snow. Hollow hooting of owls are being heard again these wintry nights. It is nesting time for horned owls. Life has grown more dangerous for rabbit and weasel alike.

The crows were returning as we headed back to the house. Suddenly, their calls became angry, urgent. Three of them pitched wildly into the tamaracks as others arrived from all directions.

Having long listened to crows, I have learned something of what they say. It was no surprise then, when a horned owl flew from the trees, a score of crows in clamorous pursuit. For that owl the day was beginning badly, but it was nothing serious. Crows are all talk when it comes to tackling owls. That haunted hooting will surely sound through the woods again tonight.

We headed back up the hill to the house. Goldfinches, those sleepyheads, were just arriving at the feeder. Nuthatches were tugging at the suet sack. A squirrel was watching from a hickory limb. It would wait for the door to close behind us before routing the birds from the sunflower seeds.

And then there was the sun, climbing into a frosty blue sky. With their raucous reveille, the crows had awakened another day.

(01/25/78)

SILENT SNOW

Spooner, Wis. -- Snow billows through the webs of your snowshoes when you trek through the north woods these days. And the silence lies deep, as deep as the snow. As you pause in the big swamps, it seems that all life is gone. Watch for the shadows then. They are alive.

Like a puff of smoke, a snowshoe hare appears from under a spruce and floats airily away. Soon after, another shadow becomes a deer, then two; then three. The last looks back, more curious than alarmed. It is a burly-bodied buck. You can imagine the rack of antlers he wore last fall. He swings his head and follows the others up a hill, through the pines.

Deer are still moving quite freely in these parts. Where it lies unmoved by wind, the snow is two feet deep, fluffy, without a hint of crust. But still farther north, beyond Sarona and Hayward, the snow heaps higher. There, deer trails have already become deep, narrow ruts which will hold the whitetails until spring. Or until death, which may arrive first in some deer yards.

However, along the many miles this reporter has trekked this week, most wildlife appeared to be faring well. Burrowed under the snow, ruffed grouse are enjoying ideal roosting conditions. One exploded out of a drift right at my feet.

Snowshoe hares abound in many of the swamps. Although there is no closed season on the species, they are now quite safe from gunners. The webs which human hunters wear are unwieldy in those alder tangles.

But why not come to see for yourself?

One of the areas visited this week was the Slim Creek deer yard off the Birchwood fire lane, some 20 miles east of Spooner. It was one of those crisp, bright, subzero days when tiny frost crystals flitter down from branches. The very air glittered in the sunlight.

There were places where weed shadows were so finely etched against the snow that they looked like delicate Oriental pen and ink drawings. Dainty too, were the twinned prints of a hunting weasel and the tinier ones of the hunted mouse.

When I followed a coyote onto a little lake, my snowshoes suddenly sagged. Dark stains spread behind me as I quickly turned toward shore. (Be warned that springholes are common, and slush underlies the snow on many northern waters these days).

My already heavy feet were still weightier on the return trip, for slush had swiftly turned to hard chunks of ice on my webs. Soft birdsounds followed me. A brook murmured as I skirted near. But every sound was muffled by that deep, white silence.

And at day's end, I discovered, I was somehow more rested than tired.

(01/30/76)

FEBRUARY

OUTFOXING WINTER

When the cold is keen, whetted by the wind. When it slices through the night like an icy scythe until all life lies still. When even the currents of the creek are quieted and the tamaracks seem to shiver in the silent swamp. How then, does wildlife endure?

Quite well, it appears.

Wild creatures adapt to winter in many ways, and, while they may not always feel cozy, they seldom suffer more than occasional discomfort from the cold.

Man's efforts to cope with cold weather often seem inept by comparison. Who else has to shovel snow, struggle with balky vehicles and labor to feed the fires we huddle near?

The fox which regularly patrols our woods made no tracks last night as the mercury shrank into a ball at the bottom of the thermometer. Reynard was lying low, probably underground, although he can survive subzero temperatures by simply curling up, sheltered from the wind, protected by dense underfur hidden in his sleek pelt. Feet and muzzle are tucked close to the belly; then blanketed with his tail.

I have seen foxes slumbering soundly on the snow -- especially after February nights when the have been running in the light of their mating moon.

The rabbit dares not sleep so deeply. But vulnerable as it is to tooth and talon, the cottontail's tender hide is a shield against stabbing cold. Its fragile fur is as warm as down.

Of course, the coats wild animals wear in winter are quite different from their summer garb. That is most evident on the snowshoe hare and weasel, which don white robes for winter, and on the deer, which change from summer's russet to winter's gray.

However, there are more important changes. Woolly undercoats trap body heat, and their insulating qualities can be increased with a twitch of skin muscles which fluff the fur still more. Birds can do the same thing with their feathers.

Most animals feast in fall to lay on fat for winter. The fat is valuable as reserve fuel for lean times -- and most critical, of course, for animals which rely on stores of fat during long winter sleeps. However, fat is a poor insulator, compared to dry, fluffy fur or feathers.

Deer actually grow fatter hair for winter. Their thin summer coats are replaced heavy ones made of coarse, hollow hairs. Combined with the deer's winter underwear, the whitetail's gray garb is superbly warm. A deer can sleep on a snowy bed for hours and scarcely melt a snowflake beneath it.

Maybe hibernators have a better answer. Of about 70 species of mammals known in Wisconsin, about a third "hole up' to escape winter's worst. There is some dispute on the definition of hibernation. It is a question, literally, of degree.

Many animals, like the fox and squirrel, are briefly inactive during severe weather. Others, like the raccoon, take long snoozes but may stir and take strolls during thaws. The chipmunk arises and nibbles at its winter stores from time to time, but rarely peeks outside until spring. The bear spends most of winter in torpor, but awakens drowsily at times.

In deep sleepers like the woodchuck, temperature, pulse and breathing rates are much reduced. A body temperature as low as 32 degrees Fahrenheit has been reported in a hibernating ground squirrel.

Its tissues are kept from freezing by the salt and other antifreezes in body fluids.

In humans, a temperature lower than 86 degrees usually results in death. We are warned that violent shivering is a sign of killing cold. Hypothermia. Yet a wolf -- or a dog -- can shiver through sieges of winter weather with no serious damage. By agitating the muscles, shivering is a way to generate body heat, but it works far more effectively for some other creatures than it does for us.

For wildlife then, winter sleeps are probably not as much escapes from cold as they are measures to conserve energy when food is scarce. With ample food available, even such escapists as migrating birds are willing -- and able -- to winter around our backyard feeders and park lagoons.

Winter can kill, to be sure, when deep snow walls the trails in overbrowsed deer yards, when hard crust bars grouse from warm roosts in the snow or when an icy glaze seals buds from hungry beaks.

Mostly though, there is no reason to feel either smug or sorry when an Arctic wind is snatching the smoke from our chimneys. Odds are that the squirrel, curled in its den, sleeps just as snugly as we.

(02/02/76)

RIVER REFLECTIONS

The river rippled over remembered stones, its dark currents carving at icy borders. Goldeneye ducks rose on whistling wings as the dog and I descended the steep, snowy bank.

And in that moment, 20 years fell away.

As my springer spaniel bounded through a drift, I could see my old Brittany doing likewise. Standing there, I remembered a younger man, wondering at much of what he saw, and trying to get it all down in his notebook.

I spent some memorable years there, along the Eau Claire River in Eau Claire County. We lived within sound of the rapids. A ruffed grouse drummed within sight of our doorstep in spring. Deer gorged on acorns in the ravine behind the house. An old bank beaver greeted me with resounding tail whacks each time I waded into his domain.

Walleyes and smallmouth bass were caught near the rapids and muskies were met in the deeper pools. Sheepshead, mooneyes and channel catfish were often taken from the lower stretches.

It has been a long time since I tried it, and I'm told that the fishing isn't what it used to be. Still, the river is there, scenic, unchanged, reflecting steep, stony banks and tall pines.

Maybe we despair too soon. My optimism has been renewed while hiking the woods this winter. The tenacity of wildlife is a marvel, even in public wildlife areas where hordes of hunters tramped not long ago. You may see only tracks, but they tell that squirrels still scamper there, and deer are browsing, and more than enough rabbits remain to renew the cycle.

Nor do we find only rooster pheasants, survivors of plantings, on those hunting grounds. The dog often flushes hens, native birds, surely seen and spared by many hunters last season. To me, they are evidence that most hunters do abide by the laws.

It buoys my spirit too, to see ducks on virtually every creek and spring pond. Although it has been a mild winter, they have endured some bitter nights to stay with us.

Nature is resilient. I realized that anew as I roamed along the river. Residential development has crowded close to the old trails, but the steep banks and wild bottomlands are a different world.

A fox had hunted there during the night. Its tracks were woven among those of rabbit, squirrel and mouse. There were fresh beaver cuttings in the river birches. A bald eagle was circling over the treetops. All was much as I remembered.

I learned many a lesson on those paths years ago. There are many truths to be learned there still.

Like, give nature a chance -- any chance at all -- and a man, or musky, *can* go home again.

(02/04/75)

THE SHARPSHIN

There had been a sound from somewhere. I stopped to scan the sky. Nothing. The horizon was a blank, gray screen. But in the next instant an image flashed over the trees. It was gone in a flash, but the picture lingered in my mind's eye as I sorted out the details:

Sharpshinned hawk! That much was easy. Any veteran birdwatcher would have recognized the dashing flight of an accipiter in that spark of time. And the small size eliminated the Cooper's hawk and goshawk.

And besides, we had met before.

But what had I seen in his talons? A dark body with a slash of red. It couldn't be a redwing in February. A starling, torn and bleeding. That was it.

I whistled for the dog and turned back up the trail. Behind the house, evening grosbeaks were flying down to a hopper of sunflower seeds. Chickadees were at the suet. For a while now, such as they would be safe from those sharp eyes and talons. But tomorrow, the hawk would be hungry again.

Bird hawks are, for me, the most difficult predators to accept around our country home. Yet, I must admire that handsome little sharpshin for his absolute audacity and independence. Alone, unloved, he huddles on his roost while nights grow bitter cold. The darkness echoes with the hollow calls of owls. They might kill him if they could catch him napping.

By day he often watches from ambush. he perches at the edge of the woods, on a route that other birds take from their roosts to the feeders.

179

He does not discriminate. Nor does he fear. Although only the size of a slim pigeon, he will strike down far larger birds if hunger demands.

Because they are most abundant, small birds are his usual marks. Finches, siskins, juncos, jays....the entire list would be as long as the lines at our feeders.

But he does not always win a race. I watched him launch an attack one recent morning. Short, rounded wings and a long tail give the sharpshin a combination of sprint speed and maneuverability which few birds can match, but this time his target was one of the mourning doves which have chosen to winter with us.

The hawk's timing was off by one wingbeat. Quickly outdistanced, he returned to his perch, seeming to shrug as he resumed his vigil.

Whatever one thinks about the way he makes his living, the sharpshin is a beauty to behold. There is a blue sheen down his back, and his sleek breast is shaded with cinnamon.

His presence has caused mixed feelings of delight and distress elsewhere in our vicinity. In the woods across the road lives an ardent birdlover who even took an injured bluejay to a veterinarian not long ago. She shuddered when I mentioned that our bird feeders were making hunting easy for the lurking sharpshin. Nonetheless, she was thrilled when I showed her the killer, waiting on his favorite perch.

"Oh, but he's so pretty!" she exclaimed.

I suppose we must put things in perspective. There are many doves and sparrows and finches, but sharpshins are nowhere abundant. And we have only one.

So, even as he brings death to our yard these bleak, cold days, the sharpshin makes the woods seem more alive.

(02/07/76)

WOODPILE WARMTH

Some wit once observed that a man is warmed twice by his woodpile -- once when he makes it and again when he burns it. Either that observer couldn't count or he had never fired a woodstove with fuel of his own making. The way I figure it, every stick of firewood represents at least six warm-ups. A cord of it is the caloric equivalent of a month on a Florida beach.

Let's hike down to the woods and I'll show you what I mean. We'll follow my snowshoe trail to the last remains of an immense burr oak. It was felled late last summer after standing dead for a year.

In September, the chain saw lopped the smaller branches into stove lengths. Hot work on Indian summer days. Then, on two frosty October mornings I returned with ax, splitting maul and wedges to sunder chunks of the bigger limbs into manageable pieces. Four of those limbs were themselves as big as mature trees As I labored, the pungent odor of fresh-cut oak hung in the air and perspiration streamed down my back.

Another day was spent with tractor and wagon, hauling the wood closer to the house. It was stacked next to rows of older wood which would be used first. The new pile grew to 12 feet long, as high as I could reach. I needed no jacket to turn the November wind that day.

Still lying in that corner of the woods was most of the huge main trunk, along with those odd chunks which resisted splitting because of knots or contrary grain. They would be tended to later.

Meanwhile, the woodpile has been dwindling. Our stove has a hearty appetite. It will consume a 50-pound armload of wood every three hours during the bitterest weather. The main woodpile is 67 steps from the door, and, since we keep only a small supply in the house, several wood-fetching trips are required daily. It is invigorating exercise, sure to warm you in the middle, even while you're freezing around the edges.

A basement woodbin would be convenient, but we prefer not to store firewood indoors for long. Most of ours comes from trees which have succumbed to old age and disease and are host to sundry spiders, carpenter ants, wood borers and centipedes. Most insects are evicted as the wood is split, but a few are inevitably brought in, to revive as the wood is warmed. Therefor, our stove gets cold cuts.

I thought about those hard-to-split chunks one recent day. It was crackling cold, but the wind was still and the distant sun glared coolly. Down the trail then, to dig those recalcitrant chunks from the snow. The cold had hardened the fibrous wood, turning any remaining moisture into flinty ice. It was no task for an ax. Embrittled by bitter cold, the thin, sharp blade might be chipped by the frozen wood. In subzero weather, a heavy maul and big iron wedges are called for.

After a few swings of the maul, my heavy jacket was hanging on a nearby limb. A few more, and my stocking cap followed. While breath frosted on my mustache, my brow was damp with sweat.

Some chunks fell apart at the first stroke. Others resisted stubbornly as the wedges bit ever deeper. You always know when you have won. The wedge announces that the wood has yielded. Instead of clanking dully when struck, it suddenly rings exultantly.

Some of the winter birds consider that sound to be a dinner bell. Convivial little chickadees gather nearby. Downy and hairy woodpeckers flit closer. Nuthatches watch, upside down, from neighboring trees.

Maybe the nuthatches remember tidbits they hid while the oak still stood. Tucked under the bark I've found sunflower seeds carried from our feeder and kernels of corn from a neighboring farm.

But mostly, the birds are waiting for cold-numbed insects to be exposed by the wedge's work. Sometimes a chunk yields fat, white grubs. This day's efforts opened a labyrinth filled with big, shiny ants.

Birds were already fluttering down to feast as I shouldered the maul and trudged back up the trail. I smiled, glad to do a favor for those who add so much life and color to the wintry scenes outside our windows. A cardinal whistled. I whistled back: "What che-eeer!"

Making firewood warms you many times and many ways. Sometimes it even warms the heart.

(02/12/85)

WINTER'S TOLL

Crows arrive in the dimness of dawn. Vague shadows drifting through the early mists, they alight silently in tamarack tops, darkly etched there, as on frosted glass. Then a raucous reveille. Crows making an announcement.

Another day, bleak and gray, has crept across hill and hollow and settled sullenly into the frozen swamp. The dog whimpers impatiently as I reach for boots and coat. He bounds ahead as I start down the trail.

We meander through the woods, inspecting a brush pile which is a hideout for rabbits, visiting hollow trees which harbor sleeping squirrels and dozing bees; then heading for the creek and the cattail patch. And all along the way, we tally survivors of another winter night.

Ducks, looming as large as geese in the fog, leap from the creek at our approach. Six black ducks and a pair of mallards have been wintering there. The springfed waters rarely freeze, but following a subzero night, only a narrow, steaming ripple of current remains. I wonder why the ducks would want to stay. And how the kingfisher can cope.

Why a kingfisher chose to winter with us is a mystery. Why would he perch on a shivering willow limb, watching those dark, cold currents, when wings could carry him swiftly south? But at least he has a snug roost, hidden from the wind. His shelter is a curving tunnel dug into a steep, sandy bank. A kingfisher couple raised a brood there last summer and the adult male has stayed. His rattling call is not heard this morning. Perhaps, wisely, he is sleeping late this frigid morning.

At the edge of the tamaracks, we find what the crows had announced:

184

Stained snow, tufts of fur, peppered brown and gray. A cottontail rabbit has died during the night. How did the crows know? Upon awakening, did they remember cries in the night? By what conjuring then, did they find this very spot in the first light of a misty morning?

Other questions are more easily answered: A fluff of brown, soft as down, lies on the snow nearby. Owl feather. Finely webbed to hush the wind. The rabbit heard no warning rush of wings when death swooped from the darkness. Convulsing in fright and pain, it struck one small feather from the attacker's breast. However, the deed was quickly done, and nothing remains to console the hungry crows.

Satisfied that all this is history, the spaniel bounds away. Tattered cattails shed blizzards of seeds as he bulldozes through the swamp. He discovers a trail of wet prints where a muskrat has recently ventured from the creek. Pursuing the scent back to open water, he plunges in, but not for long. Steaming, he paws back to shore and shakes vigorously; wagging happily. Great fun, that.

There is a wooded knoll at the edge of the swamp, a vantage point where we often stop to look and listen. Beneath one of the knoll's oaks, the dog stops to sniff at a scattering of feathers, gray, white and blue. Remnants of a sturdy black bill confirm identity of the victim and a fibrous pellet, regurgitated from an owl's gut, reveals the killer.

Damn.

Add the kingfisher to this winter's toll.

Farther on, a pheasant crossed the trail since our last visit. However, the dog's nose reports that the tracks are old. It is time then, to head back to the house for breakfast.

The place where the rabbit died gets no more than a glance as we circle back. It has told us all it can. As we head up the hill, I reflect on differences in perspectives..

There was a cold, quiet evening not long ago when my wife and I sat by the fire, listening to a duet of owls, perched just outside. Horned owls with woodwind voices, hooting a harmonious roundelay. I recall how it pleased us.

But we did not think then of the rabbit, shuddering nearby.

(02/17/75)

THE CRUEL MONTH

Like shadows rising before the sun, falling lightly, darkly upon the snow, crows come at dawn.

Yesterday they still called querulously from the tamaracks. Wary, weighing fear against famine, eyes agleam with the gold of corn they saw strewn across the snow. Soundless now, they fill ebony beaks with nuggets of grain and steal away. Unseen, they think. The house is still.

Times are as lean and cruel as a rapier's blade when crows venture to the very eaves of our country home. February can be a sword -- bright, cold and hard -- thrusting deep where life is most vulnerable.

Margins between life and death are narrow in the woods these days. And subject to sudden change. A thin crust of snow helps the rabbit flee the fox. A thicker crust makes the deer easy prey for the coyote. A crust thick enough to bear a deer's weight will allow a whitetail to reach fresh supplies of browse. At the same time, a roosting ruffed grouse may be trapped beneath the glaze.

Even there, just outside our windows, the toll is told. Rabbit tracks are fewer each week. A redtailed hawk watches by the hour from the same high perch, saving strength for the appearance of any cottontail still living furtively in the marsh.

Fate turns on small things. Possibly it was the hawk that cost one of our squirrels its tail. And it was because of that squirrel's misfortune that crows could fill their craws with corn this day.

We don't usually feed the squirrels. Their winter stores should be ample, for there are many oaks and hickories in our woods. And maples too, with sweet buds for tonic as spring approaches. So, when the rascals started raiding the bird feeders, I installed squirrel guards.

One recent day, while watching squirrels trying to shinny up to the sunflower seeds, I noticed that one of them had only a stub of a tail. Now, a squirrel without its proud plume is a pitiable thing. It isn't only a matter of appearance. The tail provides balance in climbing and jumping. It is a parachute for long leaps, a parasol for sunny days and a muffler for warm slumber in a winter den. Squirrels even talk with their tails, telling stories as expressively as a fisherman's hands.

But perhaps of paramount importance to the squirrel is the defense its tail affords. Sometimes squirrels approach potential danger tail first, keeping the plume between the body and the possible hazard. That bushy tail offers a poor grip for tooth or talon, but it may become a casualty if an attacker gets too close.

Compassion welled as I watched that stub-tailed wretch trying to clamber over the metal guards I'd placed on the feeder poles. So I made another feeder and filled it with corn. Just for squirrels.

But even where food is plentiful, there is conflict these bitter days. The hairy woodpecker gives way to the bluejay at the suet box. The nuthatch waits for the downy woodpecker, while the chickadees quietly watch for their turn.

Junco, sparrow, goldfinch, starling, purple finch and cardinal. Each knows its rank, and fights will flare if any shows impatience with the peck order at the feeders.

So too, at the squirrel feeder. Fur flew whenever Stubby was interrupted or crowded. Until one morning when blood stained the snow at the feeder and made a spattered trail to the trees. Had Stubby been victim or victor? Days passed. Squirrels continued to come to the feeder, but all had tails. I was prepared to write an obituary this very day.

But then, up from the woods, sprinted a squirrel without a tail. I mean, it looked even shorter than before. Maybe it was just because Stubby's body had grown so fat on that diet of corn. Or was it something else? When she sat on her haunches I was almost certain. Stubby had been readying a nest for a litter of young.

The waning weeks of winter often are harsh in the wild. Yet, even as life seems to flicker most feebly, new flames are being fanned in the horned owl's nest, in the fox's burrow, in the seeds beneath the snow.

And in a hollow oak on the hill behind the house.

(02/25/71)

THE LAST GASPS

An opossum, content to camp for a time in a burrow behind our house, has crept away in the cold to seek company of its kind. It won't be long now, until bumblebee sized 'possums are groping to their mother's pouch. And, as they sip of life, winter will gasp its last.

It dies hard, does winter. It flails the budding bush; flings stinging snow at the advancing sun. It causes deer to shrink in the cedars and juncos to huddle in the woodpile.

But now there is a moan in winter's howling; a sigh in its silences. And, as if to seek some solace, some sympathy in its waning weeks, winter has also been showing some winning ways.

There were, for example, the pictures framed by our windows in the woods one recent morning. Each twig was glazed, sparkling in the rising sun. Branches were filigrees of silver and crystal.

And then there were the sheen and shadows on snow drifts, sculpted by fingers of the wind. Then a sunset of frosty fire, silhouetting distant farms. Then moonbeams etching shadows on shining snow, and the dark, fuzzy forms of rabbits bounding past the house.

Another morning, fine snow swirled like smoke in the wind, accentuating scarlet branches of redosiers in the marsh. Curled oak leaves, tugged at last from their moorings, sailed over the drifts, looking like little brown galleons tacking across a frothing sea.

And after the storm, a rainbow bridged the pale blue sky.

Such were the wiles that winter worked, while weaving the illusion that all other seasons are vanquished, buried. And the woods do seem dead. Snowy hummocks bulge in the marsh, like graves for the blooms which winter slew. The tamaracks are skeletons, and the shaggy hickories, bark peeling, seem surely to have succumbed. Even the hardy cedars look rusty, lifeless.

But life is stirring. Tiny blazes struck by woodpeckers show it glowing in the red-brown underbark of the hickories. Look closer and the cedars seem subtly greener. And there is a fullness to the maple buds; an expectant yellow gleam in the willows.

A cut would reveal that turpentine is already trickling in the tamaracks. Before the frost has left the swamp, before the tamarack's needles sprout, its flowers will bloom. They are tiny ornaments -- bright yellow spheres borne by the males; scaly buds of scarlet, tipped with bright green, displayed by the females. But there are few who slog through icy swamps to witness the shy wooing of tamarack trees.

There are other signs that winter is failing. There is an expectancy in the manner of birds visiting our feeders. Seldom vocal in midwinter, they are tuning up again. More species are appearing too. Tree sparrows and purple finches have joined the regulars -- the cardinals, juncos, chickadees, nuthatches and assorted woodpeckers.

A flock of cowbirds has appropriated a neighbor's feeder, and mourning doves, which stayed close to the village mill all winter, are ranging widely again.

There is a question in the call of crows these days -- the first overtures of courtship, I believe -- and a lone redtailed hawk seems ever more restless as it sweeps across the sky.

It dies hard, does winter.

But the beat of spring is being felt in the bellies of 'possums. And in the hearts of men.

(02/27/67)

THE TAMARACK'S TIME

That the old tamarack's time had come could no longer be denied.

There were the romantic scamperings of squirrels in the woods just beyond our windows, and a rooster pheasant had been seen starting to strut around a hen. Each day the oaks were barer, their tenacious brown leaves yielding at last to fattening buds. The leaves skittered across sun-glazed snow until, as the sun warmed, they lay still, etching deeply into what remained of the graying drifts.

And there were snow fleas. Had there ever been so many? The drifts became alive with dancing specks. The tiny leapers tumbled into depressions in such numbers that they formed shimmering black puddles, like pools of fresh tar.

Clearly it was time to fell that tree. It was not a thing which would wait until spring.

Some will understand how it is. Even if one owns acres of trees, some -- or perhaps one -- will evoke special sentiment. The old tamarack was one of those. Massive, towering, aloof from the rest. Each of its lower limbs were the equal of other tamaracks huddled in a nearby swamp. It lived in the marsh with cattails for its nearest neighbors and its roots drank from a seeping spring. It was the patriarch of our lowlands; shade and shelter for countless generations of creatures. Now it was very old. And dying.

Two years ago, when others were being draped with verdant veils of spring, the upper limbs of the old tamarack remained naked, later to parch in the summer sun. Then last spring, only the lowest branches bore

192

foliage. So it was inevitable. When the marsh was frozen, the tamarack would be toppled.

However, in winter, when all tamaracks are shorn and shivering, the old one looked as alive as any. Its boughs bore the winter's snows as always. So I waited.

But then, quite suddenly, it was apparent that the ice was weakening and the snow shrinking and the creek swelling. And it was time.

There was a chain saw in the garage. I had used it to cut browse for starving deer in the snowbound north woods during a hard winter. A marvel of sorts, it weighed only six and a half pounds, easy to tote on snowshoes and a real beaver for work. It seemed a shame to attack the old tamarack with such a machine. However, there comes a time when sons are too busy being both boys and men to find time to spend on the far end of the old crosscut saw. So the little snarler was carried down to the marsh, along with ax, bow saw and wedges.

The massive trunk was cleared of limbs as high as I could reach. Then the notch was cut to tell the tree which way to fall. And finally the fatal cut was begun. Coarse, red-brown sawdust sprayed across the snow.

It did not go easily. It swayed, lifeless limbs grasping at the breeze, teetering on the narrow hinge of wood left between trunk and stump, groaning sadly. It fell with a great sigh.

A chickadee scolded as my wife and I piled shorn branches along the trunk to create a giant brush pile. The dog chased a rabbit past us as we worked. I could fairly see the cottontail making a mental note of the new refuge appearing in the marsh. However, the rabbits already had many places to hide, so a match was struck. Flames crackled and black smoke puffed from sizzling sap.

But the fire soon fizzled out. So in a way, the tamarack endures at its old stand, and tracks tell that the rabbit has already moved in.

Other tracks reveal that raccoons are roaming and skunks have left their dens. They predict that the bittern will soon be heard in the marsh; that there will be redwings hovering over the cattails and herons flapping sedately along the meanders of the creek.

The grand green symmetry of the tamarack will be gone, but our windows now frame broader scenes from the marsh and the creek . Important things happen there. Things as significant as rockets rising to the moon.

Ann Morrow Lindbergh, writing in a 1969 issue of Life magazine, summed up that sentiment in an account of a visit to Cape Kennedy with her husband Charles, of Atlantic solo flight fame.

After watching the launching of Apollo 8, they visited the adjoining wildlife refuge and recognized a symbol in a lone heron flying over the marsh:

"We realized with a new humility, born of a new pride in man, that without the marsh there would be no heron," she wrote. "Without the wilderness, the forest, plowed fields, there would be no breath, no crops, no sustenance, no life, no brotherhood and no peace on earth. No heron and no astronaut. The heron and astronaut are linked in an indissoluble chain of life on earth."

So even now, a tiny tamarack has poked from the settling snow down near the spring, beginning its own journey to the sky.

(02/28/69)

MARCH

MARCH MEANDERS

Meandering tracks of skunks are common now where snow still lies in the woods. Where they are going on their nocturnal strolls not even the skunks seem to know. Their trails are uncertain but their meaning is clear enough. It is the approach of spring which stirs the skunk from its snug den on frosty nights.

Inevitably, some stroll onto highways and become traffic victims. They fume at such a fate, and (much as it may distress poets) that is the first scent of spring.

Outdoorsfolk amble around almost as aimlessly as winter wanes. Rabbit hunting and sturgeon spearing end in February and it is near time to get our ice fishing shanties back to shore.

The later winter doldrums pass faster if time is spent reorganizing tackle boxes, tying flies, refinishing gunstocks and similar chores. Or (although I will not be thanked for this) it might even be a good time to do some work around the house.

Oil those squeaky hinges and fix those dripping faucets now, for spring will arrive with a rush, like a stream swollen with sudden snowmelt, and it can carry you away.

Suddenly there is the early trout opening on the Brule and the suckers are running in the creeks, and it is time to flee, fishpole in hand, while household chores are left undone.

Such behavior tends to give fishermen a bad name. Ask the wife of any angler who has meandered through March and she will tell you just what that name is: Skunk.

(03/01/64)

SPRING CREEPS UP

Spring was spied creeping up behind the barn the other day. It ducked, but a cardinal saw it too. And cheered.

A neighbor's old red barn and neat white house are framed in the west window of our kitchen. Size diminished by distance, the buildings are like a calendar picture -- especially when silhouetted at sundown. And the view is a kind of calendar too.

Winter is when the sun sinks far south of the barn, casting long shadows across the snowy fields. E.B. White, a longtime contributor to the New Yorker magazine, must have had such a view when he wrote:

"I am always humbled by the infinite ingenuity of the Lord, who can make a red barn cast a blue shadow."

Each winter day, the shadows shorten as the setting sun inches closer to the barn. When at last it slips behind the old hip roof, winter will be gone. Although the sun is still falling short of that mark, each day it takes longer aim and comes closer. Such things are not unnoticed in our woods.

Mallards, paired, have been splashing into the creek. A cock pheasant has been crowing in the swamp. A clutch of eggs, frozen, has been gathered from the hen coop. Frost rims the entrance of a fox den on icy mornings, telling of the vixen now nestled there, waiting. Soon there will be new whimpers of life in the earth.

Most insects still slumber. Bees huddle in hives and carpenter ants doze in tunneled tree trunks. However, springtails began cavorting when the sun's steepening rays softened the drifts on the north slope behind our house. "Snow fleas" folks call them. They appeared like a million specks of soot. And then they danced.

"Fleas? Will they get on people?" asked my wife in mild alarm when I called her out to look. No, I assured her. The poor snow flea has a terrible time getting anywhere. Curling its tiny tail against its belly, it straightens with a snap and vaults a fraction of an inch into the air -- all in the hope that it will land in a better place than the one it left.

The next morning they were all gone. Spring comes early for snow fleas, but their joy is brief.

In fallow fields, now mostly free of snow, wooly mullein leaves still wait for warmth. However, there is a fresh green look to the mosses in the marsh; a new sheen on mottled hepatica leaves in the woods. There are signs that sap is seeping, swelling buds and giving sunny tints to willow twigs.

It was still a winter sky we watched through the kitchen window early this morning. Thin clouds seemed furled to distant telephone poles, like the reefed sails of a frozen fleet. But later, as the sun slanted into the west, the clouds became flutters of white, like shivering bloodroot blossoms on a spring eve. And then the sun sank behind hills of violets and fields of prairie rose.

Distance is deceptive in the winter air, but surely that is spring drawing near.

Over there...in the sunset...just beyond the barn.

(03/05/68)

BEGONE WINTER!

Winter, somebody ought to tell you: You've really worn out your welcome around here.

And it's not just us softies, groaning about fuel bills and shovel-sprung backs. I've been poking around in the woods and the folks out there have just about had it with you, Old Man.

Just listen to that cardinal, singing to the meter of dripping icicles, urging spring to hurry. That should give you an idea.

Then there's the cottontail living in that big brush pile. The pup rousted it out of there the other day, but it circled right back. The rabbit knows that the little spaniel is no threat, compared to others who wait nearby, night and day.

There is the horned owl with owlets to feed when March arrives. And the fox, who hunts alone these days while his mate suckles new life in the den.

I followed the tracks of the fox this morning. It had circled the brushpile, sniffed along a fence row, meandered through a field of corn stubble; crept to a corner where briars were bent beneath a drift.

A pheasant rooster had been huddled there for the night. Its gaudy remnants were scattered on the snow.

You have to be a persistent hunter to provide for a family this time of year. And a pretty careful rabbit or pheasant if you're to survive until spring.

I hiked through a stand of cedars. The snow was so soft and silent underfoot that the trees could be heard sighing with relief. A week ago they bowed to you, Winter. They bent, imploring pitifully, beneath your heavy blows. Now, their burdens shed, they are straightening their tortured spines. Your cold heart won you no friends there.

You linger too long, Winter, and even when your touch seems softest it is like a cat's paw -- quick and sharp beneath.

Hiding from such perils, the cottontail remains in its brushpile refuge, gnawing bark from the protecting branches until they gleam like bare bones. Winter, that rabbit has had it with you.

Horned larks have returned. Inconspicuous, they are rarely recognized as new arrivals when they flush from the roadsides. They never some to our feeders, but glean seeds exposed as the graying snow recedes. Seed eaters run less risk by rushing spring than do such birds as swallows, which rely on insects. But they are all pecking at your heels, Winter.

Pairing is evident among the ducks which wintered on our creek. Mallards and blacks, they flew as a single flock until recent days. Now they travel in twos. They're telling you something, Winter.

Geese are pointing the way too. I watched you push them back last week. They complained loudly from the cold, gray sky as they flew before the storm. And now they are back, regrouped for another assault on you Winter. Take heed of the message in their calls.

But in case you've missed it so far, allow me to translate:

Begone, begone, you dirty old man!

(03/05/74)

REDWING'S RETURN

Come fill your cups, my friends, to celebrate. To drink to spring.

Forget the calendar, the equinox, the clocks. It is only the first week in March, but consider these exhibits:

*A redwing blackbird trilling in a tree.

*A meadowlark boasting from a fencepost.

*And just look at us! Who does not feel spring in their steps on days like these?

The blackbird departed last November in a storm of wings. A long, dark cloud of its kin swirled shrilly from the marshes on a brittle, gray dawn. They gusted through the trees and then were gone. That was a long time ago, at the start of a cold, hard winter.

Spring seemed still a long way off when I left the house this morning. A cold fog lay leaden on the land and on the spirit as the dog and I began our morning rounds. Crows, dark and silent as shadows, floated through the misty woods. Ducks that wintered on the creek flew by unseen, wings whispering, restless for a change of scene.

As we rambled, the sun rose, turning the fog into a silvery veil before casting it aside. Wet tree bark and sodden reeds, so drab at dawn, suddenly glistened with beauty. And then a redwing sang.

There he was, all right, perched on a willow, flashing his colorful epaulets; pumping out bubbling notes in duet with the rippling creek. It had been nearly four months since that reveille had sounded across our marsh.

Oh yes, there have been other signs: Some geese arrived the other day, and purple finches have abandoned our feeders. There are flashes of new color in the goldfinches' feathers and chickadees are whistling again. But, if your home is on the rim of a marsh. the redwing is the true touchstone for spring.

More redwings will soon arrive. All males. For a week or two, they'll gather noisily in communal roosts, the throngs fragmenting each dawn. Every bird then claims a tiny circle of the universe for the mate he awaits.

There will be haste to pair and to weave nests once the brown hens arrive. There is a schedule to keep. The young should be hatching at the time when insects become most abundant.

Exhibit Two, that meadowlark, was all puffed up in a sunny pose along a country road I took to town. He too, must hurry, for to nest in that field will mean to race against the haymower.

For the goldfinches, life is less hectic. Their courtship will be much longer. Not until midsummer will they build shallow nests in the bushes. Not until they can bed their eggs in thistledown and feed partly digested thistle seeds to their gaping young.

But whatever your timetable, a redwing had a message for us today. And a meadowlark backed him up.

Come fill your cup with the heady wine of spring, my friends. It's time to hold a wake. For winter.

(03/08/73)

MARCH MUSINGS

There is a scarlet bird in a tamarack top, singing, singing. An exultant answer comes from across the creek. Aglow in the first glimmers of day, the cardinals aren't merely cheering the arrival of another dawn. They're proclaiming a victory. We've made it all the way to March!

Spring things have been happening in our woods lately. True, there was a recent morning when fence posts wore new stocking caps of snow; when cedars appeared to be posing for Christmas cards. But a downy woodpecker, not fooled by that wintry scene, was tacking love notes to a hollow tree.

Although his message was tapped out in code, its meaning was plain. As clear as the whistled duets of chickadees flirting in the holly; as obvious as the actions of an attentive mallard pair, paddling down the creek, wakes shimmering like quicksilver in the early light.

I can tell you that a raccoon has begun his roamings in quest of romance, and that he has a sore foot to show for his trouble. Whether it was the result of a rebuff or not we can only guess, but he retreated to his den for a couple of nights after painting a pattern of red footprints in a lingering patch of snow. Apparently the wound was nothing serious, for the tracks revealed no limp.

Skunks have also resumed their wanderings, giving the horned owls some easier marks than our surviving cottontails. It's apparent that the rabbits remaining in the marsh are not the easy pickings they were in midwinter. It has been some time since the dog has found the scene of a cottontail's demise during our morning rounds.

No canine's nose was needed to reveal where an owl struck a skunk one recent night. The site still reeked. Owls have no sense of smell and are not dissuaded by a skunk's fumings.

Other hunters still come nightly. A lone fox has been searching the tamarack swamp. Perhaps a vixen, grown heavy, lingers at a den for his return. Like horned owls, foxes couple in winter and the young arrive in lean times.

But now there is only March, the month the sun makes its longest leap northward, hurdling the equator. Days will be nearly 90 minutes longer when April arrives. There may yet be times when winter grips hard; when the calendar seems unconvincing. But believe:

From treetop vantage points, cardinals have declared that spring is just yonder, and hurrying our way.

(03/10/80)

THE WAKE-UP CALL

The sound filtered faintly down to the dark, warm world where the chipmunk had wintered. It was beckoning...insistent. The slumbering chipmunk heard and stirred. Tiny heart quickening, he uncurled and crept along a dim corridor, past a shell-strewn storeroom, to a widening where his burrow turned abruptly upward amidst the roots of an ancient oak.

Dazzling light danced on the walls of the hollow trunk where the burrow ended. Blinking, the chipmunk paused there to stretch and to listen. Yes, spring's song was in the air. He scrambled to his doorway and peered outside, eyes and ears now doubly alert.

We saw each other at the same time, for I, too, had left my bed to seek the new sound. From the topmost twig of the tallest tree in our woods came the trill of the first redwing of spring. The sound swelled as others fluttered down to nearby limbs or swayed on tattered cattails in the marsh. The chipmunk took their notes as a pronouncement:

"Chup-chup-chrrrr!" he agreed. By the chipmunk calendar too, spring had come. There was no time to dally then, for even a chief chipmunk must make his March calls on time. It cannot be doubted that the chipmunk in the oak wears the ranking stripes in our woods. He owns the most luxurious of chipmunk abodes, and would surely be evicted if weaker than another of his kind.

Also, in the way of chipmunks, he is wise. He was not aroused, as some kin may have been, by the rallying cries of crows. He ignored the calls of the first northbound geese and paid no heed to the optimistic whistles of cardinals -- all making premature predictions of winter's end.

He did not respond to loud reveilles from our bantam rooster, which stalked past his tree daily, or to the answering cock pheasant in the marsh. He waited through the tune-up time, listening for the first movement of the symphony of spring.

There was no reason to emerge earlier. He'd laid away ample stores of seeds and nuts, to be nibbled between long snoozes. So he had slept with one ear cocked, waiting for the proper sound. When the redwings called, he knew it was time.

He was further aware that lady chipmunks would be awakened too. And it is better to let the birds do it. In the chipmunk world, the prince who kisses a sleeping beauty is apt to have his nose bitten.

The woods looked barren, even barer than when the chipmunk last saw them in the fall. The wind tugged at a few brittle leaves still clinging to the oaks. But in addition to the trilling redwings, the lilting song of a meadowlark now sprang skyward, riding away on the warming wind.

The chipmunk hesitated no longer. Tail high, he scampered down the hill and out of sight.

(03/14/66)

AFTER SPRING RETURNS

Like dark wisps of smoke they streamed across the distant sky, tugged, tattered by the March wind. No form, no pattern told what they were. An old voice whispered in my mind:

Wild geese on the horizon. And spring....and spring!

Wind chafed my cheeks as I stepped from the car to watch, to listen, along a country road:

Just listen to them! Urging, challenging, exulting....

Look at them! Surging across the ice blue sky, formations broken by their own haste and the buffeting wind.

Hundreds of them. Too many to be denied. Now winter must retreat.

Has ever any man heard their arrival without quickened pulse; watched them without his heart taking wild flight to join those beating wings?

Nor are we the only ones beckoned to follow:

Arriving home, I was met by the music of a meadowlark. And at the very tip of a hickory overlooking the marsh perched a single redwing. The first. He trilled his challenges as flocks of his fellows arrived in low, undulating flights across the fields.

Shoulder patches as bright, as red as the setting sun, they alighted in noisy confusion in our woods. In the morning, the drab and silent marsh would be alive again. The new arrivals, all males, would be staking territories amid frayed cattails.

But all of that was two days ago. Now winter swirls in veils of white just beyond the window where I write.

The winter birds are at the feeders. Juncos, goldfinches, redpolls, purple finches, woodpeckers, nuthatches, chickadees and jays. And their frenzied feeding foretells more winter on the way.

A lone cardinal is searching the deepening snow for spilled sunflower seeds. He looks somber, for all his bright feathers. He has been alone all winter. Just yesterday his plaintive invitations filled the woods, so sweetly that he surely will not be denied.

After spring returns.

A few bright promises are still to be seen. Male goldfinches, olive drab all winter, shine more golden today the yesterday. They will become as bright as summer sunbeams.

After spring returns.

But today the blackbirds huddle in naked oaks, quietly viewing the whitening marsh. Silent too, are the crows floating by in the storm, like shadows on a foggy sea.

And somewhere north of here, those geese are grounded, gabbling about the weather.

Whatever it is they are saying, I'm sure I'd agree. But I promise not to grumble further about this climate.

After spring returns.

(03/14/72)

SPRING YEARNINGS

Cattails, shaggy with age, were casting ragged shadows across the creek as the dog and I approached on our morning stroll. Wood ducks, dabbling just around the bend, splashed aloft with whistles of alarm at out arrival. The resonant call of a hen mallard arose from the reeds. A cock pheasant crowed, and was answered from deeper in the marsh.

And then there were waves of exulting geese rippling across the sky, calling to something wild and free, deep within me.

But I don't have to tell you how it is. There are some things, some joys, some yearnings, which all humankind must share. And such a thing is spring.

Pussy willows were appearing above remnants of sodden snow in the woods behind the house. Redwings trilled. Meadowlarks lilted. A downy woodpecker drummed an accompaniment to the plaintive notes of mourning doves.

But I don't have to tell you how it is as April nears ... how breath is drawn deeper and pulse throbs stronger when wispy clouds stream across a thin blue sky, how your steps become lighter when robins flutter down to greening grass.

The little juniper trees were standing erect again along the trail. Bowed by winter's first heavy snow, they had remained bent, even after January thaws had eased their burdens. They seemed to cringe, as if waiting for the next of winter's blows. Courage to stand straight again came only after a veery arrived to join the cardinals in morning song.

There's that old feeling when chipmunks appear again to scurry up

209

trees and scold the dog; when squirrels peer from hollows where blind, hairless young are already stirring restlessly in the nest.

I watched a blackbird rise to attack a passing crow. Although the redwing does not yet have a nest or mate, old rivalries have been renewed.

Reluctantly, we turned back on the path, treading silently on soft brown leaves. The dog watched mournfully as I headed down the driveway, called by commitments in town. But you know how it is.

During the walk from parking lot to office door, the wind felt cold and raw. Yet even there, in the concrete canyons of the city, a promise of spring somehow pervaded the air.

A man stood on a corner near the Rescue Mission. Shoulders stooped. Hands clenched in pockets of a baggy coat. Chill wind tugging at the cuffs of his thin trousers.

A colorful piece of paper fluttered into the gutter. The man caught it; studied it slowly. It was a brochure carelessly cast away by a visitor to a sports show in the nearby exposition center. It described a place where waters sparkled and loons laughed and fish splashed.

The man folded it carefully and placed it in a pocket. Worn shoes flapped against the cold pavement as he walked away.

Spring stirs yearnings in every heart.

But you know how it is.

(03/16/76)

MARCH PROMISES

Frost lingers in long morning shadows, still sparkling on grasses brown and bent. Meadowlark music swells from fields. A cardinal calls new notes from the creekside. Lusty cheers have given way to soft questions; sweet invitations.

Reflections of red dogwoods shimmer in the creek. Feathers from preening ducks swirl in the currents.

A rooster pheasant crows imperiously from the marsh; then flushes at our approach. Three hens follow. It appears that they have made a choice. Another suitor is seen sulking in the dogwoods. Jays betray his presence. It is their way to betray anything that hides or moves furtively in their domain.

Paired mallards dabble where the creek meets the lake. Nearby, crows alight on whitening ice and drink from a widening pool of black water. They take flight noisily at the distant cry of a redtailed hawk.

Morning air is fresh as mint. The clamor of geese rises in the south; ebbs in the north.

A squirrel spirals up to a leafy nest. A profusion of hickory hulls attests that he has wintered well.

Littering the trail too, are caps doffed by acorns and shreds of bark blazed by woodpecker bills. And tufts of fur from a cottontail rabbit to tell that not all have survived the winter in this woods.

In the marsh, green spears of skunk cabbage appear amid glazed patches of old snow.

There is a faint blush of life in the tamaracks. And a redwing trills high in an aspen, announcing that he has already staked out a territory for a mate, soon to arrive.

Why, one wonders, are buds near bursting in the topmost branches of that tree, while those nearer the roots are still tightly closed? Can it be that, even in trees, this is a season that rushes to the head?

My notebook is scribbled full of jottings and questions such as these. But all are summed in a single word.

We call it spring.

(03/18/72)

SPRING DAWN

Dawn was just peeking under the window shade when the old dog padded into the bedroom to nudge me awake. I squinted at the clock. Only 5:54 a. m.

"You're six minutes early," I mumbled, snuggling deeper under the covers. He whimpered urgently. "Maybe he doesn't feel well," my wife said.

The dog panted impatiently as I shuffled into the hallway, still buckling my belt. He pranced at the door as I pulled on my boots. The reason for his excitement was apparent as soon as we stepped into the still, chill air. Geese calling! Hundreds of them silhouetted against the still-gray sky, formations pointed like giant compass needles. Canada geese, northbound, shouting of spring.

The old dog watched wistfully. There had been some good days when the sky was filled with geese and he remembered them well. But it was no time for nostalgia. He eagerly took the lead as I set out on our morning rounds.

Chickadees were whistling their pure, two-note tunes of spring as we hiked the trail down to the creek. Sodden snow lingered in the shady hollows, but spears of new grass appeared on a slope exposed by the sun only a day before. The old dog nibbled the greens, savoring them as a spring tonic. His gait quickened; his step seemed lighter as we moved on.

Now the eastern horizon was spreading a red carpet for the return of the sun. A quintet of cardinals cheered. Those five scarlet cockbirds shared sunflower seeds at our feeder all winter, paying scant attention to three demure hens which waited their turns. Now each chesty redbird was boasting loudly, insulting his erstwhile buddies and serenading the ladies -- all at the same time.

Such exuberance set the redwings to trilling in the marsh, rehearsing for the impending arrival of their females. The first male arrived on March 1 -- some two weeks ahead of schedule in our latitudes. When winter pounced back three days later, I wondered if that over-optimistic blackbird was being buried under the drifts. However, when the sky cleared again on March 6, he was again bubbling bravely over the winter-worn cattails. Within a week, he was joined by a throng of others. Yet I am sure that he is the one holding the highest perch in the popples bordering the marsh. He sang there as we hiked past.

We rounded a field where winterbent grasses revealed runways which had hidden mice from fox and hawk. A killdeer called. A mourning dove cooed. Surely those were sounds of spring.

Ah, but we have too often been betrayed. Skepticism comes naturally at such times, in these latitudes. More proof was sought.

Then, so distant that I could not be sure, I sensed the staccato sound that would be the clincher. I had to know for sure. I called a friend who owns a much larger marsh, five miles distant.

"Have they come back?" I asked.

"I haven't been outside yet," he answered with a yawn.

"Well, put on the coffee pot, I'm coming over to see."

A flock of mallards winged over as I pulled into his driveway. I stepped out and listened. More geese were clamoring. And then there was that old music again, louder, closer, until the majestic musicians themselves were seen suspended in the now-azure sky.

The sandhill cranes were back. Spring had come early. And this time it looked as if it meant to stay.

(03/18/85)

JUST ASK THE BIRDS

How can we know that spring has come? Where are the signs when ice still glints on the quiet creek; when gaunt deer huddle in yet deep snow?

We have ever looked to the birds for word of winter's end, and they say it has arrived.

The ducks which wintered on the creek are winging away as pairs. A rooster pheasant has been strutting through the alders, proudly displaying resplendent spring plumage. Crows mill restlessly above their roosts in the pines. The song of cardinals lilts through the frosty morning air.

Perhaps birds know spring's signs best because they are of the sky, steer by the stars, know their meanings . Perhaps they sense that spring is really a magic potion of particles caught in the heavens. Surely they see that the Big Dipper has turned upside down, to shower the earth with the elixir it holds.

It will arrive as droplets which daub the dogwood shoots and willow buds, in trickles which make music in the creeks; in torrents which tear at winter's bonds. And then as splashes of color; as jewels of dew.

Though the sun may yet seem distant and cold, 11 first magnitude stars sparkle in the early spring sky -- more than in any other season. Birds cannot count them, or name them, but they know them. They are the guiding lights for northbound geese. They bid the redwings to return.

Men may believe that spring emerges from the earth, from bursting buds and flowing sap.

Birds know that the season is cupped in the sky.

(03/22/65)

THE SOUTH WIND

The south wind bustled into our woods today, whistling of spring and sweeping up some of winter's litter.

It tugged at leaves and heaped them at the bottom of the hill, where the marsh begins. There, tousle-headed cattails got a thorough shaking, sure to stir the frogs slumbering amid their roots.

It blustered at the debris of winter's last, shattering storm, and whispered to hepatica leaves, still hiding under the damp, brown duff of autumn.

It carried a chorus of Canada geese, and buffeted the flock back on course when its leader tried to detour westward.

It buoyed spirits and lightened steps as the spaniel and I started our regular look-smell survey from field to swamp; then through the oak grove to the creek. The stroll became a romp.

We chased a cheeky chipmunk up a tree, rustled a brushpile to awaken a rabbit, and watched a pair of teal -- new arrivals -- splash down in the flooded tamaracks.

We poked in middens of hollowed hickory shells, investigated a woodchuck's den, listened to the distant crowing of a rooster pheasant. Two cock cardinals began a vocal duel that became a duet. A meadowlark sang from a fencepost while robins discussed the wind's promise of rain.

Each morning now, the sound swells. At first light there is the peenting of a woodcock. Flickers and woodpeckers arise almost as early. Then the larks, redwings and robins awaken.

More voices and new tunes are heard each day. A wood duck's whistle has been heard, and even grackles are trying to sing. However, even in top voice, a grackle sounds like a rusty hinge.

Each day willow buds bulge bigger and grass grows greener. I wonder then, how our winter birds know that snow still lies deep in the north, and that it is not yet time to go.

Evening grosbeaks still crowd the feeders and purple finches are still among the small scratchers on the lawn.

But the south wind beckoned them today. Tomorrow they may be gone.

(03/25/76)

APRIL

TURKEY TRACKS

Snow rasps and squeaks underfoot this morning, but I am unsympathetic to its complaints. It doesn't belong here. It has overstayed its leave. It is the second week of April, Easter past, and still the lakes are icebound; still there is snow.

Winter has its good points, but everything has its limits. The snow came early last November and it stayed, deepening, drifting. Soon it crusted enough to keep grouse from snuggling on bitter nights; enough to bear the weight of roving dogs and hungry coyotes and wolves. But deer broke through and foundered, wearied and died.

It has been a cold winter, with the mercury shivering at the bottom of the thermometer. A mean winter with lacerating winds. A long winter. Stubborn. Reluctant to depart.

Redwings trill at the fringes of the frozen swamp this sunny day, but they have been back for nearly a month. Eager, foolish birds, they have somehow endured Arctic days and knife-edged nights to stake claims amid the tattered cattails. Redwings then, aren't truly signs of spring this year. They only speak of hope that winter is waning. We must look farther for assurances. How about a hike through the Elk Mound swamp?

As Wisconsin wetlands go, the swamp is large. It encompasses hundreds of acres of marshland and flowages, interrupted by tangles of alder, copses of willow and popple, islands of oak, birch and maple, and a towering pine here and there.

Even in the depths of winter, access to the islands is risky. Flowing springs create weak spots in the ice and I have sometimes broken through, gasping as icy water embraced my belly and muttering expletives as my boots sank into the pungent muck below. A few times, I have even taken the plunge while wearing snowshoes, extricating myself with exercises that might confound a contortionist.

Now the ice is old and weak, rotting under arbors of winter-bent reeds, more treacherous than ever. Rubber-booted, I risk a crossing at a narrow channel to arrive at an island of about 10 acres. I know that the island often harbors ruffed grouse and deer, and always squirrels and rabbits.

Today the snow tells that there has been little traffic since the last flakes fell a week ago. However, there are the wandering tracks of a 'possum and purposeful prints of a hungry coyote, and a surprise: Recent turkey tracks.

The dimensions of the splayed prints leave no doubt that an adult tom has passed this way, but what has attracted him to the island? Even if last fall's acorn crop had not been a failure (which it was) the deep, crusted snow would have kept turkeys from scratching up any sustenance anywhere near.

His tracks lead to a big pine, where they mingle with a maze of smaller tracks. So the gobbler has found a harem. Or was it the other way around? The pine appears to be a regular gathering place. A roost tree. Its dense greenery would help conserve radiant heat as the big birds huddled on winter nights.

The snow shows where the gobbler has danced and strutted, wingtips dragging in the drifts. So turkeys too, are impatient for spring.

There are other signs of such frustrations: Furry pussy willows, lured by brief March thaws, now shivering in the wind. A pair of bluewing teal dallying at a bend in the creek. Crows carrying nesting materials. An icicle hanging from a storm-shattered maple limb.

The icicle reveals that sap was running strong in the old maple's veins during the thaw. I snap it free and taste it. It is only faintly sweet, but it leaves my hands sticky when I toss it away.

But soon the syrup kettles will be steaming in the sugar bush again. Soon now, stirrings in bellies and burrows, in sapwood and seeds, will burst into life. Soon spring must return with a rush.

Turkey tracks in the swamp attest that it is so.

(04/09/96)

PORTRAIT OF AN ANGLER

Picture a fisherman. What do you see?

The store clerk might envision a lunker, to be landed with the latest in technology and tackle. The wife, perhaps, sees an idiot who spends a fortune and a lifetime trying to outwit creatures with brains no bigger than peas. The preacher may see an empty space in a pew on a summer Sunday.

Cartoonists draw him as a ridiculous oaf whose antics are interrupted by long siestas afloat and ashore. He is usually depicted with outstretched arms, caught in an enormous lie. But if you would find a true fisherman you must put such caricatures aside, or search in vain.

A real fisherman is the idol of more idle anglers. But more than that, he is an example for humanity. Statistics show that, when the chips are down, 10 per cent of the fisherman will catch 90 per cent of the fish. The course leading to such skill is simple -- but not easy. True artistry in angling requires endless labor and love -- two things which many of us give too grudgingly, if at all.

Fishing should be approached with an inquiring mind and a poet's soul, for it is both science and poetry. The true angler studies the subject seriously. He learns about the fish, their needs and desires. He perceives the community of things in the water and the world.

He is ever an explorer, an adventurer, even on a mill pond.

There is no caste system on a creek. Not among real fishermen. Instead, the angler is judged according to his skill and his sportsmanship.

The world needs more of both.

A liar? Call him a prophet. Maybe the one that got away wasn't quite *that* big, but it will grow.

Imagination is vision, and this world could use more of that as well.

(04/16/64)

WEDDING MUSIC

The wedding music has begun. For now it is a march, with drums and fifes. There is the resonant boom of the prairie chicken, the muffled beat of ruffed grouse and the tattoo of the sharptail's dancing feet, all setting tempo for the trill of the redwing and the lilt of the lark.

It grows each dawn, quickening in cadence, swelling in volume, until bursting into spring's full symphony at April's end.

Everyone knows that birds sing of love, but their courtships are not all song. Birds not blessed with beautiful voices woo in other ways.

A pheasant rooster sprinted into view as we looked out a window during breakfast this morning. He stopped, bowed, and puffed his pretty plumage. Then the reason appeared.

A demure hen poked her head above the weeds, glanced sideways at the strutting suitor, and darted away (to my wife's delight). The hen was careful, however, to run neither too far nor too fast. She halted when overtaken, coyly watched the rooster's dazzling display; then fled again. As he persistently pursued, she finally led him into the privacy of the dogwoods..

Nearby, blackbirds were flashing their bright epaulets. A crow flew over, carrying a twig which might be offered as an invitation -- and the beginning of a nest.

Even the oft-scorned English sparrow is a saucy-looking suitor when he puffs his black-bibbed breast and chirps for his lady.

Some birds, including several species of the larger waterfowl and birds of prey, marry for life. However, most mate only for the season.

And that dalliance in the dogwoods was destined to be even briefer. The pheasant rooster will seek several mates; then go his unfettered way while the hens tend their nests.

Sharptailed grouse go romancing quite differently. The boys invite the girls to a hoedown. Then each hen makes her choice of one of the fast-stepping specimens on the dancing grounds. She takes her time about it too.

The hen may attend those dawn dances for several days, remaining a spectator. When she finally does curtsy to a partner, her participation is brief. She soon flies off to prepare a nest, while her beau remains to dance on -- and enchant another if he can. The courtship of prairie chickens is similar, except that the hens are the audience to a remarkable roundelay of drums.

The ruffed grouse, on the other hand, is a solo performer. He returns to the same mossy log as dawn nears, day after day, there to beat his breast in invitation. Since each hen is receptive to the sound for only a short period each spring, the cock grouse spends many hours strutting on a lonely stage. He drums at short intervals for hours at a time.

Some ducks are already paired when they wing northward. Others wait until they've reached their nesting grounds. Dabblers, like mallards, usually pair early. The drake rises almost upright in the water, nods low, and utters low grunts that must sound like love talk to the hen.

Divers, such as the redhead, typically throw their heads back as they call to the hens. The hooded merganser spreads his crest. The ruddy duck fans his tail.

Matrimony is usually taken seriously, even among species which mate only for the season. I have seen two mated pairs of bluewing teal attack a preening bachelor drake -- and both sexes seemed incensed at his intrusion.

The woodcock, a bird of many offbeat habits, starts romancing as night descends. He rockets into the air, spirals high on whistling wings; then plummets down as wind twitters tremulously through his feathers. He lands again and again on the small patch of damp, dim earth he has claimed for himself, always hoping to find a bride in waiting. Failing that, he utters an odd "peenting" call for a couple of minutes; then takes to the air again.

Many other birds resort to aerial acrobatics as they're courting. Bobolinks sing and display on the wing. The marsh hawk swoops in undulating flight to delight his lady. The nighthawk towers high; then falls from the sky, ripping the quiet evening air with sound as he pulls out of the dive.

Each sound, harsh or sweet, is a note in the rapturous chorus which will diminish all too soon. Songs become solos as the birds become busy rearing their young. Yet, there is a brief time each day of spring and early summer -- just as the first light breaks -- when almost all of the voices may join in song. Listen then.

And if, one day in July, you find that the music has grown fainter; fuzzy with young voices, it only means that the honeymoon is over -- and that a new generation is tuning up for the next spring serenade.

(04/17/65)

STEELHEAD FEVER

Brule, Wis. -- Dawn arrived as a bright silver stripe across the eastern horizon. There was just a hint of pink in the first light. It could have been an omen, for those are the very colors of the Brule River's brawling steelhead trout.

Ice crackled underfoot in a boggy stretch and a cold wind gusted through the trees as we walked down to the river.

"It feels almost like a day in fall," remarked Mark Senn, somewhat wistfully.

Mark is a steelhead fisherman. He loves April because it is then that steelheads leave the icy depths of Lake Superior and enter tributary streams such as the Brule. But Mark loves November more, for then there are also big brown trout which charge upstream to spawn in fall.

Steelheads are rainbow trout which spend much of their lives in the big lake. There they lose most of the rainbow's colors. They look like molten silver with shadings of gray. Still, they remain river fish at heart, so they run up tributaries to spawn in spring.

There had been conflicting reports as to what the Brule's trout were up to. Some said that the females were spent of spawn and were heading back downstream. Other reports indicated that they were still surging upcurrent with their precious cargos of pink eggs.

I'd met Mark Senn and Henry Houle in Brule the previous evening. They had driven up from Menomonie after Mark finished his mail route there. Arriving at 6:30 p. m., each had caught a couple of four-pounders during the next two hours. Mark had also lost a much bigger one.

"We got there just at the beginning of the period," explained Henry, who fishes only during the "periods" indicated by the solunar tables.

"I kept at it after Henry quit, but the fish had stopped biting," Mark added.

Henry announced that the next major period would begin at 5:30 a. m. That's why we were at the river as the next day dawned. Mark speared a tiny sack of trout eggs on his hook and flipped it into the current. Almost instantly, there was a strike. Soon an 18-inch steelhead was gasping in the net.

Henry moved upstream and soon was tied to a five-pounder which almost took him swimming before he subdued it. Then, just that quickly, it was over.

"The period is past," Henry declared. "There will be a minor one at noon and a major one at 6:45 p. m."

It was time, anyway, for me to warm my fingers over the typewriter and move on to other appointments. But I would be back. The steelheads of the Brule beckon too strongly to be ignored.

Anglers may number 1,500 or more on the Brule on a busy day. Wally Niemuth, the state fish biologist on the river, says that the total annual catch wouldn't allow even one of those big trout for each of them. While a few take limits, many are luckless.

"I'll tell you what this fishing is," said Henry, shivering as he took just one more cast. "It's a disease."

"And there's no known cure," Mark agreed.

For a sick man, he looked happy.

04/18/63

AFTER SUNDOWN

Now the sunsets speak of spring.

Summer days die in flares of color. Autumn sunsets are splashed with a bold brush. Bright winter days end in cold, neon glows.

But now soft pinks and purples are edging puffs of clouds, as though the early woodland flowers are reflected there. And you can hear the day, spent of catching sunbeams, sigh and yawn.

As if on signal, trilling redwings fall silent in the marsh. A meadowlark lilts its last notes and flutters from fencepost to field. A rooster pheasant crows a goodnight from across the creek. Finch and flicker, robin and bluebird, cardinal and dove, all hushed as the colors fade and darkness deepens.

A pair of mallards, swooping silhouettes, pitch over the tamaracks and splash into the swamp. And then the night is awake.

The woodcock begins its dainty dance in the final flickers of light. A series of metered "peents;" then a dizzying climb into the darkness followed by a twittering, spiraling descent.

For a month, beginning in March, that rotund brown bird implored spring to hurry. Even in gusting rain, in snow, in sleet, he persevered. And now he is rewarded. A demure hen has been spellbound by his strange serenade.

The peeper who leads the frog chorus was another who nagged at spring's dallying. The fragile-looking little frog peeped persistently, even as ice crept across the marsh again one recent night.

Day and night, in the treetops and under the earth, the pulse has been quickening. While digging in the garden one recent day, I uncovered nine tiny turtles struggling from eggs. Painted turtles. Their bellies were as bright as newly minted pennies.

Carried to the creek, they swam off without a backward glance. Some though, may one day be back to dig nests in our garden.

And just today, from a fence wire, a bluebird complained as the pup and I passed by. It seems that the tree swallows, arriving earlier, had claimed all of the vacancies in the vicinity. A trip to the workbench then, to build another birdhouse. He can claim it in the morning.

Tonight we watch a little brown bat's acrobatics in the light from our windows, wondering what kind of insects he finds there. And we hear the bittern begin his hollow, pumping calls from the marsh. There is a certainty to that sound.

The sunset spoke of spring. The night shouts that it's true.

(04/18/73)

SPRING TRICKERY

Shadbushes shivering at the edge of a marsh, their white blossoms mingling with swirling snowflakes. Hepaticas huddled on a hillside, petals tightly furled. Mayapple leaves wearing white stocking caps.

Winter deserves a cold welcome when it returns in late April. Frogs fall silent. Birds perch morosely in budding bushes. Sheep, newly shorn, bleat unhappily in a neighbor's barnyard. Icy fingers of wind have been strumming funereal tunes on fence wires and plucking eggs from swaying robin nests.

But even a blizzard can't hide the futility of winter's dying frenzy. The world is too full of spring. Bursting buds are spraying a rosy mist in the crowns of red maples. A cloud of green hovers in the tamaracks. Bloodroot blossoms bow in patient wait for the sun's return.

Strawberry leaves shine amid sere stems of last summer's lushness. Swamps spill over from a bounty of snowmelt and spring rain. Ducks dabble in flooded fields. The herons are here.

Spring's early arrival has brought many songbirds our way ahead of schedule. Now the migrants tarry, uncertain of the season. Warm winds brought them this far, but the angle of the sun cautions them against traveling too far, too fast. Even more than the weather, intensity of light -- the length of day -- influences the timing of bird migration.

But whatever nature's system, it is not foolproof, so winter is no stranger to early birds and blossoms. Like us, they must shrink and shiver. And endure.

(04/25/68)

234

THE OVERTURE

It begins in that chill stillness before dawn in early spring. When wisps of mist hang over the marsh. When the stars begin to dim. Listen:

"bup-Zeemp . . . bup-Zeemp!"

The woodcock is singing, pumping his rotund brown body in a dance of romance. There is fervor in his voice, for somewhere near must be a mate, listening; watching in wonder.

She is a third bigger than he, with a build like a softball. Her ears are near the base of her knitting needle bill and her shining dark eyes are near the back of her head. But to the woodcock she is all beauty.

And, less than 75 yards away, is a rival, peenting the same promises.

This is the overture to a daybreak concert which fills fields and woods with music in spring. With his bill as a baton, the woodcock is both conductor and soloist at the start of the symphony.

On a downbeat, he rockets into the sky, circling for a time on whinnying wings before hovering, perhaps 300 feet up. Then strange, tremulous notes tumble down through the darkness. A cascade of sweet chirps falls to earth as the bird is dives dizzily, like an airplane out of control, zigging, zagging, wind whistling through his wings. Amazingly, he pulls out just in time to land safely on his launching pad and begins strutting and peenting anew.

The bird's oddball appearance and antics have earned him many nicknames -- hokumpoke, mudbat and siphon snipe among them. Timberdoodle is the one used by many of his admirers, and it somehow seems to fit. His voice is truly hard to describe. It has a buzzy, nasal quality which some say sounds more like an insect's call than a bird's. Naturalists describe the sounds as "peenting" for lack of a better word. Joe Linduska, a longtime friend and widely-known wildlife biologist, once remarked that the calls sounded like "the eructations of a flatulent frog."

The sound is heard at the first hint of dawn and in deepening dusk -- and even at night when the moon is bright. The woodcock does not time his serenades by the clock. He only knows that the time is spring.

As the woods awaken to the timberdoodle's tune, the tempo increases; volume swells, for many of our summer birds are answering the role this early April morning. What is melody to our ears, of course, has other meanings to the birds. Mated males proclaim at dawn that they have found a fine place to raise a family this summer -- and that they mean to keep it. Those still unattached sing boasts of what fine, bright birds they are -- and brave.

The redwings arrive in bachelor flocks. They teeter on tattered cattails and trill until the brown females arrive. Then how they flash their scarlet epaulets and bubble and boast!

There were early birds this spring. A veery's spiraling song soared across the creek even as the first flocks of geese arrived. Voices of meadowlarks now mingle with the calls of our resident cardinals. Mourning doves and robins answer as pussy willows shimmer like giant dew drops in dawn's first light.

These are days when the pussy willows glow with yellow pollen and wood thrushes are piping from the thickets. Now hickory buds are as big as the ball of your thumb, and flickers are wickering and drumming on trunks of the shagbarks. Popple catkins wave where chickadees perch and whistle.

There is a rusty hue in the budding tamaracks, where crows complain about redtailed hawks soaring above the swamp, and cedars, where jays and grackles argue, have turned from bronze to green again.

Still with us are such old friends as the creepers, nuthatches and juncos. Fleeting visitors are warblers of varied voice and hue. A bluebird has announced its arrival and the first bobolink has been heard. Each day brings new notes from finches and sparrows and shorebirds. Rosebreasted grosbeaks, brown thrashers and orioles are surely close behind.

A pheasant is crowing as the first long rays of sun set red dogwoods ablaze. Another returns the challenge. Day has come. The music becomes muted as its makers begin busy hours of seeking food and building nests.

Under the alders, the woodcock is probing for worms in the cool mud. No, there are two of them -- one much bigger. After all, what lady would not fall under the spell of such a songster as he?

(04/27/68)

MAY

SPRING VOICES

It starts, sometimes, with the lilting song of a meadowlark perched on a fence post. Unseen. Day has not yet dawned, but it is spring, and days are much too short for all that the meadowlark has to do and say.

Robins then, and cardinals cheering first light. A woodcock soaring, diving, twittering. A secretive sora sounding its giddy call from the marsh. A whinnying snipe circling above.

Then sunrise and silver dew, a yellow shafted flicker slanting to earth like a sunbeam; a brown thrasher practicing its varied song, repeating each phrase before trying another.

Snow-white bloodroot blossoms and purple hepaticas on a wooded hillside; marsh marigolds glowing at the margin of a pond. Green splashes of strawberry leaves amid the brown forest duff. Bumble bees rumbling by.

As day brightens, peepers fall silent. The soprano voices of those small, pale tree frogs are among the first to announce spring's arrival. They are joined, these nights, by tenor notes of leopard frogs and the baritone green frogs. The bullfrog's bass booming is yet to be heard.

Spring begins stridently, losing shrillness as the orchestra grows. Now toads trill tirelessly along the creek. Soon the deep, pumping calls of the bittern will give a tempo to their tune.

Nature's baton is quickening. Each morning the music swells with new notes. They sound hurried, for spring is brief, and summer all too short.

There is impatience in the redtailed hawk's cries to her soaring mate.

It is time for haste. Buds are already bursting in the oak where she nests. With the same urgency, crows call from the greening tamaracks; doves from the cedars.

The frog concert swells in the swamp as dusk returns. A restless meadowlark sings to the rising moon. The woodcock is aloft again.

Dawn to dusk, night and day, Spring's voices are never stilled.

(05/01/70)

SPRING ALCHEMY

From leaden clouds, silver showers. From silver pools, mounds of gold. Such is the alchemy of spring. Marsh marigolds are in bloom.

Already the pasque flowers and bloodroots are wilting. And speckled spears of jack-in-the-pulpits are thrusting through autumn's litter. And sprigs of trilliums have appeared. And Mayapples are opening their umbrellas.

Watch closely or you will miss much of the show. Hepaticas will soon fade from the hillsides, to be quickly followed by bursts of anemones, columbines and shooting stars.

Pussy willows already have grown whiskery with age, their yellow pollen gone on puffs of wind. Red buds bulge on maples, A green haze veils the tamaracks. Ferns uncurl. Leaves unfurl.

Spring dallies girlishly through April...skipping, meandering, retreating coyly as we reach. But by May she is a woman grown, and by June a wanton. There is passion now in her pulse, her voice.

Exulting: The soprano of peepers, baritone of leopard frogs, bass notes of bullfrogs, all singing in harmony. Then the sweet calls of cardinals, the trilling of redwings; the wood duck whistling from the creek.

Inviting: Flickers bowing on a branch, wickering softly; a jacksnipe circling, swooping as if to follow its giddy notes; a twittering woodcock spiraling from the sky.

Demanding: The coarse call of a rooster pheasant, impatient summons of crows; harsh heralding of jays.

Then yielding: Hen robins huddled over fragile blue eggs; blackbirds on guard in the cattails.

Even the heron is not safe in the marsh these days. Sedately, even in haste, he flaps down the creek as red epaulets of his attackers flash angrily in the sun. He seeks a quieter pool, for he must keep fishing. He too has a mate, waiting in a rookery miles away.

Spring's promises have blossomed into love affairs across the land. Nature's magic act has begun anew.

Marsh marigolds are in bloom.

(05/02/69)

HEPATICAS

All winter the three-lobed leaves lingered, waiting under the snow. Dappled and weary-looking, they kept their posts until the first slanting rays of spring sun probed the leaf mold. Then, dying, they signaled their roots that it was time.

Furry green spears jabbed through the brown litter. So fragile were they that their tips shattered against the sunbeams, bursting into bits of blue beauty.

That's how hepaticas happen.

They arrived in our woods this week, dainty blooms hastening ahead of new leaves. Then, again deserted by the sun, they cupped pale petals protectively around pistil and stamens and waited once more.

Nearby, bloodroot leaves were unclasping, revealing the white blossoms they had been clutching so tightly. So it is time too, to find spring beauties nodding pink-veined petals in an open woods; to catch crocuses unfolding on sun-warmed slopes.

May is the month of woodland flowers -- shy, delicate things, yet bold enough to blossom while coarser plants cower in the cold earth. Some even emerge to joust with sunbeams while snow still dapples the woods, but they shrink from shade, and from the heavy hand and foot of man. They wane as buds unfurl in the treetops. In summer, ferns will bow over their resting places.

Undisturbed woods are habitat for bellwort, adders tongue, Jack-in-the-pulpit, Dutchman's britches, trillium and anemone, but not all spring blooms are so showy. The Solomon seal shelters its greenish blossoms under its leaves. A wild ginger hides its flower near the root. So look closely. And tread lightly.

The flowers of woodlands and bogs are mostly intolerant to trespasses of man. They seem to shrink from the touch. They will wilt in the hand. Trilliums are long gone from many places where they bloomed in profusion. Trailing arbutus has become rare. Lady's slippers and bittersweets are seldom sen in their old haunts.

Those, along with the Turk's cap and wood lilies and the lotus, are among flowers specifically protected by Wisconsin law. However, the salvation of woodland flowers will come not from legislation, but appreciation.

So let us gather the bouquets on film or sketch pads, or simply in our hearts. We can return then to see the cranesbills bloom as the trilliums wane. Even now the leafy rosettes of shooting stars appear, violets are pushing up, strawberry leaves are emerging. We can watch then, as colors spill into the clearings and fallow fields, increasing in variety and intensity as the sun climbs higher.

Columbine, blue flag and phlox. Wild rose, gayfeather, bergamot and vervain. Lupines, spiderworts and lilies. Foxglove and indigo. Each has its particular time and place as summer passes.

Summer days bring true bouquets, for many flowers of the fields are persistent perennials which will beam bright in a vase. Black eyed susans, cone flowers, campions, chicory, asters and daisies are among the most common.

But for now, walk softly. The first flowers in our woodlands are as gentle as spring itself. And just as welcome as the first trills of redwings and choruses of frogs.

(05/07/65)

TARDY SPRING

A brown thrasher is saying it all.

Perched in a budding oak, he sings a medley, each phrase repeated a single time before changing tune and tempo. While he is not the only songster in the woods this day, that serenade would suffice to celebrate the sudden rush of spring.

Nature is rushing to make up for lost time.. Wildflowers, long pent in frozen earth, are pushing, scrambling, to bud and bloom. Instead of appearing in their usual sequence, each in turn, woodland plants are emerging in mixed array. It is as if spring, long overdue, has come breathless, apologetic, bearing dazzling bouquets.

Hepaticas explode across a hill, like blue sparks struck from the sky. Bloodroots shine under the oaks, leaves still clasped around their stems as if huddling from the morning chill. There are sunbursts of dandelions, violets peering from tangles of greening grass; marsh marigolds strewn like golden coins amid ragged remnants of cattails.

Mayflowers parade along the path, unfurling their umbrellas for the next rumbling rush of rain. Trilliums and cranesbills, anemones and shooting stars are on their way, hurrying to take their places at their appointed times.

Such a spring is almost worth waiting for. Nature has a way of catching up. Almost. The farmer knows that for each two days corn planting is postponed, his crop's maturity will be delayed a day.

Whatever the weather, warm-blooded wildlings must run the risk. Their schedules are set not by temperatures but by position of the sun.

Even now the first crop of rabbits is venturing from fur-lined nests, a robin is hiding in a cedar, warming her eggs, and newborn mourning doves are huddled forlornly in a flimsy nest in a pine, awaiting a parent's return with a serving of "pigeon milk."

So at last spring is gathering momentum. Sunbeam and lightning, birdsong and thunder are bidding the woods awake. And to all who would listen, the brown thrasher this morning was telling it all.

(05/09/75)

THE ARROWHEAD

It was one of those mornings when the earth appeared to be celebrating another spin around the sun. Marsh marigolds glowed along the borders of the creek. Frogs chorused in the swamp. Redwings trilled in waving willows. And yes, there was that first faint scent of lilacs in the air.

But, tempting as the idea was, this was hardly a time for loafing. All of spring pulses with a certain urgency. On this day in our woods, it seemed that Ma Nature was conducting auditions. Listening to an oriole, a rosebreasted grosbeak and a brown thrasher competing for solo parts, I thought that the thrasher's lyrics said it best:

"Hurry-hurry, sweetly-sweetly, quickly-quickly..."

Truly, there is much to do in May. It is the time to wade a stream in quest of trout. Time to glide the canoe along a lakeshore and flip poppers for bluegills. Time to poke through greening woods in search of morel mushrooms. And yes, time to plant the garden.

Most of our garden was already planted, but tomato and pepper plants had been kept inside until threats of frost seemed past. In our latitudes, guessing the date of the last frost is always a gamble. However, when lilacs begin blooming I'm ready to take the risk. Lilacs know at least as much about such things as I do.

The dog sprinted ahead as we approached the garden plot. The reason was quickly apparent. A woodchuck had been eyeing the emerging goodies in the garden. Hard-pressed, it sought refuge in a slender aspen. Awkwardly, it hitched itself up the trunk, looking like a fat man trying to shinny up a flagpole. It clung there grimly, just beyond reach of the outraged spaniel.

"Let that be a lesson to you, " I warned, leading the dog away. The woodchuck looked as though he'd gotten the point. I hoped so. If he trespasses too often he might end up in a stewpot with some of the veggies he craves.

Much of gardening is best done on one's knees -- an appropriately prayerful attitude for an endeavor so filled with hope; so fraught with risk. Thus, I was soon moving along the rows like an awkward rabbit, hunching over each tender plant as it was set in place. The earth being turned by my trowel felt cool and damp, but the sun's warmth was like a healing hand. It unlimbered muscles tensed by too much time at the office.

Something grated on the blade as I dug. Another stone? Our ground has plenty of those. No, this was something different. A triangular point protruded from the soil I'd just spilled from the trowel. With quickening pulse, I brushed dirt away to expose it fully. It was a flint arrowhead. I held it in my palm, marveling at the skill which had turned a shard of stone into a thing of such symmetry and utility.

I know a few things about arrowheads. As a boy, I was tutored in Indian lore by an uncle, an amateur archeologist. And, although not a collector, I have over the years picked up an odd lot of such artifacts. Each has a story to tell. They range from a massive spear point, found on a Kansas plain where I hunted quail, to a tiny obsidian bird point discovered in the middens of a South Dakota prairie dog town.

But to find one in my garden? On land which was tilled for a century before we bought it? How many times had this arrowhead been unearthed and buried again as this field was turned and churned by plow and harrow?

Its triangular shape and notched base were typical of those used by the Woodland tribes. And, although artfully made, almost perfect in its symmetry, it was obviously intended for robust duty. Quite heavy, it was an inch wide and half again as long -- more than would be needed to down a deer. It would have required a lusty bow to propel a shaft so-armed, I knew. Especially so, if it needed sufficient force to reach the vitals of an elk, a buffalo or bear.

A thousand questions flitted through my mind. How had the arrowhead come this place? Had the hunter missed his mark? Surely he would have recovered his valuable arrow if it had remained in a fallen quarry. Where did the hunter come from? Was his village near, or was he on a long journey? Was he alone or with a party of fellow braves? Foraging or on the warpath?

Had the hunter fashioned this arrowhead himself, or had he obtained it in trade with an artisan in his or another tribe?. The flint from which it was made was surely quarried many miles away. Perhaps in what is now Illinois.

And just how long ago? It is believed that bows and arrows came into common use in these parts something more than a thousand years ago or so. The type of projectile point I now held in my hand appeared during the same period, and agriculture began not long after.

What things would the hunter have recognized in my garden? The corn and squash, surely. But what might he have thought of me, engaged in such squaw work?

In my reverie, I tried to conjure up a conversation with him: *"Look here,"* I would say. *"I caught the fish whose innards are buried to fertilize the squash. Your people taught my people that. But I am a hunter too. I'll show you my bow. And I have arrows with heads that are sharper, much sharper, than any of stone.*

"Indeed, I could show you even greater wonders, like thundersticks which can strike down a duck in flight or a deer at great distance. But while our tools are different, in our hearts we are brothers. I would like to hear your stories, for I have much to learn from you. Far more than you could ever learn from me."

But alas, there was no response. The arrowhead had already told me all that it could. Carefully, I put it in a pocket and got back to work.

Planting done, I stood, stretched, and retrieved the arrowhead from my pocket. As I rubbed it between my fingers, I gazed into our woods and tried to picture how things looked way back then.

The kinds of trees had probably not changed much. They were still mostly oak, hickory and maple. And most of the same wildflowers still bloomed in places which escaped the plows and overgrazing. In our woods alone, there is a rainbow of blooms.

But not all was woodland when the hunter was here. There were savannas -- wide sweeps of grassy prairie maintained by fires sparked by lightning or torched by man. Buffalo and elk grazed on those Wisconsin prairies. So the arrowhead's owner may have been seeking such quarry, as well as deer and bear.

"Well," I mused, *"at least the deer still roam our woods."*

Did the hunter stop to drink at the springs behind our house? And did he pause to watch the trout in the creek? It must have been teeming with them. With a probe, I can still feel the gravel lying beneath the deep silt which now covers the bottom of the stream. Its water still runs clear, but the creek is now more to the liking of green sunfish than speckled trout.

I walked slowly back to the house. I saw that the woodchuck had abandoned the aspen, probably opting for a safer refuge in a burrow. Of course, the dog double-checked the tree, just to be sure.

The woodland chorus was muted now. The birds were busy at other things. They too have much to do in May.

My fingers were exploring the contours of the arrowhead for the hundredth time. It now felt familiar in my hand. Doubtless that long-ago hunter had done the same. I wished I knew more about him, but of one thing I felt sure:

We had much in common. We could have been friends.

(05/11/69)

MAY MORNING

There was still the breath of winter in the wind when the dog and I set out for our morning walk. Tiny aspen leaves shivered on slender stems. The creek looked cold, gray, except for the silvery wake of a swimming teal.

But despite the chill still spilling into our woods from the north, spring's signs are shining brighter at each sunrise. So we walked down a slope bright with blossoms -- blue hepaticas underfoot...shadbushes shimmering with white petals and downy leaves. Tamaracks and willows were poking their heads into pale green clouds of emerging foliage. Hickory twigs were swelling; oak buds bulging.

Swaying in a swamp maple, a redwing trilled. A robin flitted furtively from a red cedar limb as we approached. She flew to a nearby oak to watch and worry. I peeked into the nest she had just left. She had been incubating four blue eggs. One of the shells showed a tiny white pip. We left quickly.

We circled the swamp, now fringed with fresh green spears of blueflag and the shaggy heads of last year's cattails. There the dog discovered where a rabbit had died...a patch of soft, gray-brown fur... white cottonball tail.

A marsh hawk, slim, silhouetted against the sunrise, soared over the popples across the creek. A redtail screamed from a distance. The hawks seem ever hungry, and it appears, sometimes, that they must have caught the last rabbit on our holdings. But there is always another...and another.

Little wine-tinted leaves adorned the branches of the wild cherry trees and the creased leaves of gooseberries were just unfolding. Jays called. A pair of flickers fluttered by.

Because I could see over the brush, I noticed the pheasant before the dog did. A beautiful rooster, resplendent in spring plumage, was striding down the path. He paused to crow and beat his wings, but cackled away in dismay when his invitation was answered by a bounding dog instead of a demure hen. A short while later, a squirrel scurried up a tree. It watched impishly from a limb as the dog barked below. It was a familiar game.

Ferns were unfurling. Leaves of cinquefoils, vetches and raspberries were verdant against the tawny tops of last year's grasses.

Whitethroated sparrows whistled. Their notes conjured visions of granite-rimmed lakes, of spires of spruce, of laughing loons. The white throats will spend summer amid such scenes.

There was a dandelion pinned like a bright boutonniere on a green shawl of grass near the creek bank. A crow hurried over, harried by a pair of blackbirds. A cardinal sang, "What-CHEER! What-CHEER!"

But it was time to turn back toward the house. There would be just time to sip a cup of coffee before the dog woefully watched me disappear down the driveway, bound for less important matters, which nevertheless, provide paychecks.

We made one more stop at the cedar tree. The mother robin was loathe to leave. She perched nearby, nervous and noisy. Naked, pink, the first of her brood had just struggled from its shell.

There was still a nip in the wind, but spring had just taken another step into our woods.

(05/12/67)

RENEWALS

One can guess how the deer died.

A hunter stood in that clearing last fall, listening to the murmur of the little creek and watching a furtive form among the pines. He shot before he was sure; then slipped guiltily away.

A coyote came and fed on the fallen doe. It stayed nearby, keeping watch against the foxes and ravens; then gorged itself again. Hairy remnants of its scats still lie near the scattered skeleton.

Now dainty anemones wave there, taller than their neighbors, and violets, deeper lavender amid the bleaching bones. Nearby, wintergreen still bears some of its refreshing fruit -- bright as tiny, polished apples.

In the clearing and along the trail, the violets are white. Nature seems inclined to hide darker colors in the shade. The jack-in-the-pulpit is an example. The dimmer his church, the deeper purple are his priestly robes.

Where the deer died, the forest floor is dappled with dancing bits of shade. The woods will darken as more leaves unfurl. Meanwhile, wild strawberries will bloom.

Listen: A ruffed grouse is drumming -- a haunting, distant sound. It has been a hard winter for him and his kind. There was little snow in which to hide and sleep, and the hawks and owls were many. Other springs, these woods have reverberated with the sound of drums. Today there is but one. One hopes a hen will hear.

Blue jays, bright and cocky as sailors just ashore, are singing their almost bell-like spring song, "tee-lunk, tee-lunk." And it sounds like a white-throated sparrow is whistling a four-note introduction to a brown thrasher's exultations.

But come now. We can follow a hummingbird's flight to some columbines, and there will be buttercups along the creek. Choke cherries are in bloom, and cranesbills have begun to blossom amidst the trilliums.

There is a place where hepaticas hide, nestled in the roots of tall trees, and where May apples soon will bloom. There is still time to seek spring beauties and bloodroots too. But they are only the beginnings. May brings indigo, blue lupine, white vetch, merrybells, groundsels, starry solomon seals, spiderworts, and many, many more.

The doe knew all of those places. She lived in these woods for three years. Her teeth tell her age. Last spring, perhaps, she led a pair of spotted fawns down this dappled path. Probably, she drank at this bend in the stream and browsed on these branches. But whatever she took, she has returned.

Man is no different. Whatever he takes from this place, he must repay. Unless he carries it in his heart.

(05/13/64)

FINDING CLUES

The trail through the woods is strewn with clues these days: Fallen petals lie under big, veined leaves of bloodroot. Trilliums shine on the hillside. Dainty anemones surround a mossy stump like pink-cheeked children at the feet of a patriarch.

No doubt about it. Spring has been there, now and then.

Spring has been playing hide-and-seek, distracting us with dandelions while freezing our crocuses; flirting like the waves of spring warblers now here, now gone.

However, our backyard birds, from their vantage points, have apparently been keeping the season in sight. Although winds have blown hot and cold, a brown thrasher's tuneful announcements have kept time with the calendar. Perched in the very top of a big, budding hickory, the thrasher sings, exults, revels. His enthusiasm is not dampened, even as chilling rain pelts his breast and streams from his tail. You have to believe then, that spring is in full view of those bright, yellow eyes.

His example is followed by celebrations of robins, lusty whistles from cardinals, exuberant notes from a grosbeak, trills from swooping swallows. Even a sodden, gloomy dawn brightens at such greetings.

May's rains arrived too late to freshen the earliest flowers. We missed the usual blue profusion of hepaticas pushing through autumn's litter, but scattered clusters did appear and some linger still. Now the Mayapples have spread their umbrellas and marsh marigolds gleam like a pirate's booty uncovered in the swamp. Columbines are budding and wild cherries are about to bloom. Spring's smiles, although all too few, have been very fetching, it appears.

A closer look reveals that the great renewal is, in fact, well along. The woodcock still makes its twittering courtship flights, but I happen to know that the hen he serenades was already incubating eggs in mid-April. Not far from our house, two mallards are expecting ducklings any day. And down in the dogwoods, a rabbit crouches over a bowl-shaped depression. Her nest is about five inches deep, lined with her fur and cleverly concealed with dry grass. Hungry mouths reach up to nurse as she covers the place with her body.

The five hungry young are already clad in fine, gray fur, but their ears are no bigger than a chipmunk's and there's not yet a bit of cotton on their tiny tails. In just one more week, they'll look a lot more like rabbits. For now, I keep the dog away. The truce ends at the garden fence in June.

Summer comes hopping along about then too, if I rightly recall. So let's go take another look.

Yes, I guess what we've got here now is spring.

(05/17/70)

BRAZEN SPRING

I remember when spring was a lady, demure, garbed in gossamer greens, warming but slowly to the wooing of the sun. So who was this brazen hussy leaping into our woods this week? She arrived with the quiet grace of a clanging trolley car, and what an uproar has ensued!.

Every frog is about to burst his bellows. Every toad is shrilling, shrieking. There is a fury of flying and fighting among the gentlest of birds. Why, even the wildflowers are pushing each other around!

The trouble, of course, is that the wait has been oh, so long. Even hepaticas get impatient, I suppose. So, when the sun at last warmed the earth they exploded in blue showers above autumn's brown litter.

Usually the hepaticas hold the stage alone for a while. but this time others would not wait. Bloodroot and trillium, anemone and Mayapple, cowslip and columbine crowded onto the scene.

Just as suddenly, those birds that had not yet nested began frenzied flights. Every blackbird has a beakful of grass. Barn swallows are swooping into the open garage. And nearby, bluebirds and tree swallows are waging relentless war for possession of a house on a fencepost.

The swallows are a handsome pair, and I was glad to see them inspecting the bluebird house earlier in the week. No bluebirds had been around the claim the place. But then, like an electric bolt, a cock bluebird flashed from the sky and the battle was joined.

At first I thought to interfere. That bluebird would surely be no match for the swift and agile swallows, and the swallows are many; bluebirds few.

Nonetheless, the bluebird perched atop the house, pivoting this way and that, meeting every assault. The snapping of his tiny beak could be heard 50 feet away. His mate meanwhile, confident of his courage, simply moved into the house.

The swallows did not surrender readily, but hours later the bluebird was singing victoriously from his housetop.

Other squabbles have been going on in the treetops. Furious flutterings of cardinals and orioles, grackles and doves.

One pair of doves has escaped the harassing grackles. Their twin eggs lie safe in a tiny nest on a shelf in the garage. Grackles, which all suffer from guilty consciences, are much too wary to venture inside.

The earlier-nesting birds have had problems this tardy spring. Their nests were too long exposed in naked trees and scant ground cover. Competition for food has been keen too, for insect hatches have been sparse.

But now, tiny, carmine leaves are unfurling in the oaks. the hickories and cherries and maples are greening. And there is the hum of tiny wings in the summery air.

So, even if spring has awakened the woods with the subtlety of a bosun's mate sounding reveille, it is forgiven here.

Things are quickly getting back on schedule. Ruffled feathers are being preened. Jack-in-the-pulpit and asparagus spears have appeared.

If a lady is kept too long waiting, you'll notice, things happen fast.

(05/19/72)

THE POND

I had found the pond while hunting for snowshoe hares. Their tracks had led me far from the road, through a frozen marsh, to a tangle of tag alders bordering a creek. Poking along the meanders of the stream, I'd come upon a snow-covered flowage with a domed hut of sticks and mud in its midst. There was the home of the beavers who'd choked the creek with a sturdy dam. Stretches of dark water rippled darkly, both upstream and down, speaking of flowing springs. Surely a place to remember, come trout season.

I remembered when passing through the area in spring. Evening was near and thunderheads were building on the horizon, but I was weary of driving and the woods beckoned. My destination was still hours away. An hour or so of delay would matter little.

It was muggy, uncomfortable walking in waders, but pleasurable nonetheless. Tiny violets and strawberry blossoms were strewn on the forest floor, as if confetti had been tossed in celebration as spring paraded past. Fiddlehead ferns shook clenched fists at my trespass, while trilliums beamed welcomes from a shady knoll. At my approach, a ruffed grouse hopped from his drumming log and walked stiffly away. Challenges -- and invitations -- of others reverberated in the distance.

The hike seemed farther than I remembered. But finally there was the pond. I slipped quietly into the water, welcoming its cool clasp around my legs, pausing to watch and listen for a while.

One of the charms of trout fishing is that a wader can sometimes approach creatures which are otherwise very wary. A person in the water is often regarded as benign. Curious birds watch from overhanging limbs. A mink may swim by. Deer will come to the banks to drink.

Standing still, I reveled in the swell of birdsong, sorting out calls of myriad warblers and cheery chickadees, spiraling notes of a veery, jackhammer signals from a woodpecker. A bittern spoke. It is one of the most remarkable sounds in nature, almost impossible to describe: "Ooongga-choonk! Ooongga-choonk!" It has a liquid quality which some say sounds like a pump. Or like a stake being pounded into soft mud. Few venture to haunts where bitterns are heard these days. Even fewer see the stocky brown-streaked bird. Statue still it stands; rapier bill pointed skyward, blending beautifully into its marshy retreat.

Then began the giddy giggles of sora rails, secretive gray-brown birds which could soon be seen scurrying amid reeds and flooded alders, calling nervously as though each was lost. A heron, ready to call it a day, took off from the pond's edge and flapped sedately away to its rookery, perhaps many miles away. A pair of mallards splashed into the pond. A wood duck whistled. Redwings and frogs had started trilling in chorus.

When a beaver appeared, swimming to the dam to make its nightly check for leaks, I realized with a start that darkness and the storm were both near.

I had come to the pond to try for trout, but as I turned to leave, there was a rattling sound in the alders. It was the flyrod, forgotten in my hand.

(05/23/63)

THE RETURN

The sun is sinking. Its red glow freshens the paint on the old barn and lights lamps in the windowpanes. But there is still time, as this day fades, to stroll the trails.

I have been away, to places far from home, and am now amazed at how far north the sun has journeyed during my absence. Come along and see for yourself:

A bittern's strange, pumping call is coming from the creek, and an oriole, teetering high in an oak, has raised its voice to duet with a distant cardinal.

With nervous notes, a meadowlark flutters from the field; flops back to earth with trailing wing. That old ruse tells that her four hidden eggs have hatched.

There, under an archway of grass, huddle four naked larklings. Their mouths are agape, but silent. It is unwise for little larks, bound to the ground, to advertise their whereabouts.

Nearby, eye high in a cedar, a bluejay still warms five mottled olive eggs. She slips away furtively as we approach; calls frantic alarms from a hickory limb while we peek.

A starling, working overtime, has carried a caterpillar to a hollow in a cherry tree. Its arrival is heralded by a clamor within. A bluebird flits by. It too, like the robins chirping down the hill, now has a family to feed.

On a low knoll just beyond the tamarack swamp a redtailed hawk watches from her bulky nest in an oak. And somewhere in the shadow of those same trees, the mallards must have their nest. Just now they are returning to the marsh, wings cupped, descending into the dusk.

Oh, how spring's step has quickened in less than two weeks away!

Wild strawberry blossoms gleam in the deepening dusk, appearing even brighter than the anemones still blooming beneath the oaks. And here and there the first shooting stars have opened. And columbines. And cranesbills.

There is a cloud of holly blooms wreathing the tamaracks and the scent of honeysuckle lingers in the still, evening air.

Fruit is already forming on the shadbushes. The gooseberries have tiny blooms. Grape and mulberry leaves are unfurled and the wild asparagus is branching into lacy foliage.

Mandrake buds are bulging under umbrella leaves while jack-in-the-pulpits watch from under their own arched shelters

Two weeks, in springtime, is a long time to be away.

Wary frogs fall silent as we near the creek. There, new cattail leaves stand like pickets around marsh marigolds. A fish swirls. Swallows still swoop in the darkening sky. A nighthawk appears on rakish wings.

Late for bed, a chipmunk flees from the dog and scurries up the scaly bark of a black cherry tree. That tree's white buds tell that summer is soon, but not yet. Long after the chokecherries and other kin have dropped their petals, the black cherry bursts into bloom. Seldom do its flowers know frost, and it is a rare season that the tardy tree does not set a banquet for the birds.

A woodcock is peenting now. The afterglow of the sun silhouettes his tiny form as he circles higher and higher. Then he dives, twittering and tumbling into the darkness, where he will sit a while and invite company.

The woodcock's call is an odd, buzzing sound. However, it speaks of spring to lady woodcocks. And to others who love his haunts.

Each day of spring there is a new scene on stage. I may have missed some things, but it appears that I've returned in time to catch the best of the show.

(05/24/68)

SMALL DISCOVERIES

Magenta trilliums matching the hues of wild geraniums on the wooded slope. Swordlike leaves pointing the way for blueflags along the creek. Violets peeking through matted grass, strawberry blooms scattered in the shade, golden five-fingers gleaming along a path, campions shining in a field.

The waning days of May are times for small discoveries.

Now is the time when Mayapples swell under umbrellas of leaves; when Solomon seals arch gracefully over droops of buds. Pussy toes are in bloom, miniature bunches are appearing on grapevines, and the tamarack swamp is wreathed with a cloud of holly blossoms. Nearby, green spears of cattails are waving amidst the shaggy remnants of last year's growth.

Dogwoods have begun to bloom. Honeysuckles, pink and white, are emerging on the hill. And here and there, the wild asparagus is branching into beauty. Those plants which escape picking will be at their prettiest in late summer, when feathery foliage is decorated with scarlet fruit.

These are also days of great expectations.

The brown thrasher says so with bursts of song, notes so pleasing to the composer that he repeats each phrase before improvising another. Catbirds mew duets in the early evening shade. A wood thrush pipes and kingfishers rattle. Soon now, the woods will be aflutter with the awkward flight of young wings.

And too, these are days for soft goodbyes.

The chokecherries' petals have fallen, anemones have wilted, and

266

where hepaticas heralded spring, only   mats of three-lobed leaves remain.

Little things, all. Dabs of color in life's tapestry. Yet they are more than pigments in the pattern. They are the fabric's very threads.

Communing with nature, we begin to recognize old truths.

And that is no small discovery.

(05/28/65)

ON GARDENING

Gardening is not considered one of the great outdoor sports. In fact, some otherwise all-around outdoorsmen have been seen cringing at the sight of a spading fork. It may be that some of our more elite anglers fear that we'll think they are digging for worms.

It is time then, to point out that the outdoorsman who really digs gardening will benefit in many ways.

For example, wrestling with quack grass is an excellent way to tone up muscles used in casting, and to develop the strength and endurance needed to land truly big fish.

By actual test, a single quack grass root can put up a tougher battle than a 58 3/4 pound musky. And if you don't believe it, try yanking out quack grass with your musky rod.

Another thing: A garden is the perfect disposal area for fish innards. Bury them so the roots can just reach, and don't overdo in one spot. (Of course, the more fish you catch, the bigger garden you need, which reduces your fishing time somewhat. But it all evens up).

Nothing else comes close as a fertilizer. Why, we have some buttercup squash jumping over the fence!

And you know that expensive, hand-crafted bamboo flyrod you've lusted for all these years? Go right out and buy it. Your garden will save you hundreds of dollars. (At least, I think I read that somewhere).

Gardening is good training for the hunting season too. Tip-toeing around in the cucumber vines will sharpen stalking skills. And when you can spot a potato bug skulking in the greenery 20 paces away, no deer is likely to sneak past your stand next season.

Gardening equipment can be just as elaborate -- and expensive -- as boats and reels and guns and such. However, just as you can go fishing with a canepole and hunt with an old single-shot, you can do a lot of gardening with hand tools. Our patch is small enough to manage without power tools and can be tended with no great demands on our time. Yet, it produces more vegetables than we can readily use.

I spend more time out there than is necessary, just watching the swallows swooping nearby, bluebirds fluttering down to snap bugs and bobolinks bubbling over the field. A person puttering in a garden is not a threat. A robin lands to probe earth just turned by a hoe. A meadowlark lilts from a garden fencepost.

The nearness of other birds is told in song. Oriole, thrasher and rosebreasted grosbeaks seem to be competing for top honors, and it's a three-way tie. A pheasant crows across the creek. A cardinal whistles.

From the garden too, I can hear frequent confrontations of cowbirds and blackbirds down along the marsh. The cock redwing keeps vigil while his hen is absent, lest an alien cowbird eggs be laid in the nest. But the cowbirds try again and again, and occasionally they succeed, as indeed they must. Even parasites have to work at survival.

So you see, gardening yields far more than vegetables. Like simple fishing, it offers a retreat from a hectic, more complicated world.

And where am I going with that can of worms?

Why, to transplant them, of course.

(05/28/73)

THE HARRIER

Soundless, a hawk glided past, floating bouyantly over the sweet clover. A female marsh hawk, so intent in her hunt that she took no notice of me, standing in the nearby fencerow. She settled swiftly, softly, only a few yards from my feet. Then she was aloft again, talons empty. There had been a brief scurrying under the clover. A mouse had been missed.

Circling, sailing, searching, the hawk swept near again. Surely she would now see the meadowlark's nest. It was so ill-hidden in the grass that even I had found it.

Suddenly a lark fluttered up from the field, tiny under the span of the hawk's wings, anger apparent in every wingbeat. The hawk turned away with a shrug of wings, but it was too late for a quiet retreat. The general alarm had been sounded.

Blackbirds boiled from the nearby marsh as the hawk swooped away, wings grabbing for altitude. The redwings pursued, pecking at the white target at the base of the hawk's tail. Flinching, she flailed for more speed, but each time one attacker turned away, two more appeared.

The hawk was nearly out of sight before they gave up the chase.

I watched as the hawk turned back, gliding low once more to try her luck in a field across the road. But a kingbird lived there, I knew, and she would doubtless be punished for venturing so close to his domain. I whistled for the dog and headed back to the house.

It is seemed ironic, I thought, that "harrier" is now the official name for the marsh hawk. Who was being harried by whom?

I remember that, as a boy, I often thrilled at the sight of brave little birds doing battle with "chicken hawks" (as we called them) and other such villains. How scornful were those cowardly killers, and how well they deserved what they got.

But as I grew older I became less judgmental about such things. I finally perceived that the hawk's retreat is not an act of cowardice. It simply cannot outmaneuver its small attackers, any more than a bomber could engage a pursuit plane in a dogfight. And I came to realize that there is hunger in hawk nests and bellies too.

The hawk, after all, is simply playing the role which has been written for its kind. It is for us then, to watch and learn and play our part -- and not try to rewrite the script.

(05/30/68)

EARTH SOUNDS

Two US spacecraft "condemned to wander forever" among the stars may carry recordings of voices, a baby crying, bird songs, music, animal grunts and other Earth sounds when they blast off on planetary probes this summer.

-- UPI dispatch, May 7, 1977

Stars wink awake in the deepening dusk. The moon, with half shut eye, already is squinting down at us. A whippoorwill's upbeat song is lilting to the sky. And what says that song, I wonder, if not sung to moon shadows in the marsh? What meanings have those notes unless they soar over dusky field and forest?

But then, one need not journey to outer space to find ears to which such sounds are foreign. I remember a colleague, a city man, who wanted to know why anyone would stumble through an inky night in pursuit of raccoons. He was invited to go along.

We had stopped at the edge of a clearing, listening for the hounds, when a shadowy form loomed near. It made a loud "WhooSHHHH!"

"Whatsat-whatsat-whatsat?" my companion stammered.

"Just a deer snorting," I assured him.

"Well, I'm getting out of here!" he declared. He spent the rest of the night waiting in the car.

An editor who took his son on a spring backpacking trip, complained on his return that the wilderness experience had been marred by frequent sounds of someone working in the woods. The sputterings of some kind of motor had dogged them along the Appalachian Trail, he lamented.

"Bup-bup, bup-bup, bup-pup-pupupupup-PRrrroooOOOM!" said I.

"That's it!" he declared. "What was that?"

"It was a cock ruffed grouse, drumming his love song," I answered.

People miss much joy and appreciation of nature if their ears are deaf to the language. However, my pleasure is tinged with regret as I roam the woods these days and nights. There is music for which I can write no adequate words:

There is the strumming of bullfrogs and the trilling of toads while galaxies of fireflies swirl over the swamp. There is a twittering woodcock, spiraling down a moonbeam while his hen huddles in a well hidden nest near the creek.

A chattery little wren, just outside the bedroom window, bids yellow goatsbeard blossoms to open anew each day. And there is an oriole whose nest remains hidden from my eyes, but who sings assurance that it is still there each dawn.

How, I wonder, could any recording truly capture the flute-like calls of a wood thrush from the deep, green shade on a golden afternoon? And can a rosebreasted grosbeak really be heard, except from a treetop?

Wordless though they are, such sounds speak to any who will listen and learn their language.

There are some residents of our land which I rarely see, yet they tell me when they are there. And also when they are gone.

There is no bittern this year. His hollow, pumping song is missed. But a pair of little green herons has moved in.

No kingfisher rattles above the creek this season. The one which was a year-round resident was eaten by a horned owl one winter night. Now the horned owls have moved away. Their hollow hoots are no longer heard. Instead, screech owls whinny through the night.

The bluebirds are nesting elsewhere this season, apparently having lost all battles with tree swallows which compete for the houses we offer. They have not gone far, however, for I often hear a cock bluebird whistling in our woods.

I hear a mallard hen admonishing her ducklings long before I see her leading a downy brood across the creek. The agitated voices of robins tell intruders that clumsy, speckled fledglings have left their nests.

I know of no classrooms for such teachings, no text, no videotape. But trust technology to surmount such problems:

"The spacecraft will last for perhaps hundreds of millions of years," said Carl Sagan, the Cornell University astronomer who heads the committee planning the record for the space agency. "It might be nice if someone does receive it, that he knows a little bit about us."

Sooner than that, it is hoped, passengers on Spaceship Earth will come to understand what the Earth sounds are saying.

Then we would know more about ourselves.

(05/30/77)

JUNE

IN DEFENSE OF
BLACK FLIES

A brief press dispatch recently bore sad news for wilderness lovers. The Associated Press reported that research is under way at the University of Maine to find a way to eliminate the pesky black fly. Black flies, the story explained, are known for ruining the day of many a trout fisherman.

Offhand, I can think of many things which ruin trout fishing, but black flies aren't on the list. 'Fact is, I'm inclined to place them on the other side of the ledger.

Oh yes, those little devils do bite, and their bites swell and persist and are downright discomfiting. The Maine variety, I can attest, is no worse, than those I've encountered elsewhere. In fact, black flies are not nearly the nuisance that some people are. People who want a wilderness paved and cushioned against all discomforts, for example.

When modern man pokes into a wilderness, he is an intruder -- a trespasser -- even at his best. He probably deserves to get chewed on a bit, and he often is, even if he swelters under a head net and pours a pint of repellent down his perspiring neck. It may not be pleasant, but it is a price fairly paid for being "back in."

Such places are not for those who think that "roughing it" is a drive down a gravel road. Demands for roads are heard as soon as the bugs and bogs are conquered. However, roads to everywhere will lead to nowhere. In each natural environment, everything is good for something. Historically, mankind has taken the narrow view. Tunnel vision causes us to ignore ecological relationships and often leads us into nature's ambushes.

People don't like mosquitoes, but martins do -- and dragonflies couldn't get along without them.

But aside from their benefits -- often not understood -- there remains reason to preserve space in the world for creatures we find uncomfortable.

As a matter of fact, we already know how to put black flies out of business. They breed only where there is clear, cold, fast flowing water, and man has been doing a dandy job of eliminating that kind of habitat.

If black flies help keep some places too inhospitable for that kind of encroachment, I'm in their corner. And I'm willing to take my lumps.

(06/02/66)

COMING OUT

Dripping ferns were still uncurling at the margins of the marsh. On the hillside, strawberry blossoms were bright in the gloom of a dreary, drizzly dawn. Footfalls were hushed on the rain-soaked trail.

That is why Old Ma Raccoon had not noted my intrusion. That, and the fact that she was busy getting one of her young down from the den.

Headfirst, she inched down the trunk of an old oak which has been home to generations of raccoons. She didn't hold the youngster by the scruff of the neck, as a cat would. Instead, it rode upside down, tightly curled around its mother's head. Baby squirrels are carried to new nests in much the same way.

Ma Raccoon disappeared in the direction of the creek, still carrying her cub. I crept closer and hid behind a neighboring tree, hoping to see the rest of the litter leave the den, but I was too late. I had just glimpsed the departure of the last one.

Bird-like "chirring" sounds could be heard as the young were instructed to stay close and watch carefully. Then silence. I could picture Ma Raccoon cautiously leading her little troop to adventures in their vastly widened world.

It is not usual for mother raccoons to evacuate their dens by day, but maybe she had simply had enough of being cooped in that hollow with four or more rambunctious rascals. Little raccoons are that, for sure.

The mating was late in January and the litter arrived nine weeks later in a much-used den tree within view of our windows. When three weeks old, bright eyes blinked open behind those tiny robber masks. Now, at two months, the young are ready to start foraging; to clutch slippery frogs with nimble fingers and taste of crickets and turtle eggs. There is very little, in fact, that a raccoon can't eat with relish and impunity.

The encounter was a reminder, if one was needed, that many young wildlings are taking their first wide-eyed looks at the world these days. Dappled fawns watch from shady shelters where magenta cranesbills bloom. Fuzzy fox kits romp near entrances to their dens. Small squirrels already scamper in the trees while miniature cottontails abound in the briars.

Mother rabbit is now hunched over a hidden nest to nurse another litter. It is, in fact, her third family this year. And, if she survives, she may raise two more before wearying of such affairs in September.

To make room for more offspring, young muskrats too, are hustled from their home lodges when hardly a month old. Nature demands high production rates from species which are high insurance risks. Traps and turtles, mink and a myriad of other killers -- some microscopic -- take heavy tolls of muskrats.

June is the prime month for the young of most species of Wisconsin wildlife to venture from their nests. It is a time of succulent stems, sweet flowers, swelling fruit and tasty bugs. The busy chipmunk, which still has several mouths to feed, is shucking a bonanza of juicy June bugs from their hard, brown shells.

It will be July before most young chipmunks are on their own, and even later when baby badgers emerge, but the woodchuck children will soon be wobbling to daylight to nibble greens, and tiny weasels are already being weaned.

All wildlife has schedules to keep. Thus there are fretful peepings in a hollow oak where woodpecker chicks are impatient to fly. And bumblebees droning in the purple vetch. And lessons being eagerly studied with newly-opened eyes.

Such are the signs which tell the time, if one can read nature's hands.

(06/04/70)

FLOWER WATCHING

Clouds of holly blossoms wreath the tamarack trees these days. Five-fingers scatter their golden coins in deepening shade of oaks. Columbines droop amidst pale purple cranesbills. Waxy white blooms of May apple now nod beneath umbrella leaves.

Such gardens grow where no-one tills. Planted by bird and wind, they flower in woods and prairie, dune and bog.

Spring's first fondling touch arranges the first bouquets; the iron grip of late fall frost gathers the last. Between those times, there is a succession of heady scents and hues to be found. Few seek them.

One can hardly avoid seeing wild flowers. They splash across fallow fields and daub color in vacant lots. Too often though, they are only multi-colored blurs, glimpsed through car windows; their beauty smeared across the glass like that of the butterfly which splats against the windshield.

For space explorers, speed is essential to stay in orbit. However, there are still wonders to be discovered by those who putter on the ground.

This morning, shooting stars and Solomon seals bowed to each other where a forest met a field. Honeysuckles, pink and white, painted a showy border along a country road. The wild cherries and dogwoods were in flower, and pale yellow goatsbeards were glistening with dew.

Even a slow stroll is a rapid pace for a real flower watcher. One might inch up steep bluffs to find tiny alpine blooms and breathtaking views. Or slog through cool, stained bog waters where pitcher plants hide and insects hover like haze. Or pole a canoe up a little stream which is lavender with reflections of pickerel weed.

Observing flowers, one sees other things: How bees seem dizzied by the heavy scent of basswood blossoms. How yellow pinions of a winging flicker are like sunbeams dancing through a shaded woods. How a nighthawk sleeps lengthwise on a limb.

There is a great store of folklore about flowers, and much of it is fact. All but forgotten are ancient skills of foraging for food in the forest; how to make thongs from leatherwood, use a mullein as a torch or extract dyes from root, bark or blossom.

Many common flowers have medicinal value. There are hazards in concocting home remedies from them, for some are emetics or have narcotic or toxic qualities. However, modern medicine has recognized the value of many plants, and researchers expect to find more cures in others.

Some plants which were favored fare of the Indians are too rare or beautiful to be taken as food today. However, there is still much satisfaction in gathering wild fruits, or knowing how to spice a salad with woodsorrel or watercress.

Flower names are interesting. And confusing. Often a plant is known by different names in different places, and sometimes the same common name is applied to various unrelated species. Even botanists have argued about how plants should be classified.

I like the descriptive names: Dutchman's breeches, jack-in-the-pulpit, lady's slipper; bluebells. Such names are not always attractive, however.

There is a beautiful blue, three-petaled flower which blooms in early summer in many waste places. The stem, when broken, exudes a slippery, frothy juice. Books call the plant spiderwort. Since I had never noticed any particular association between that flower and spiders, I thought it might have a more descriptive name. One day asked a Chippewa County farm wife what she called the spiderworts blooming near her driveway.

"Cow slobbers," she answered.

There is such a variety of wild blooms that identification is sometimes difficult. Standard field guides can cover no more than broad families and the most common species. Most guide books explain the names of flower parts. Once you've learned to note the structural differences in plants, you can use such clues to "key out" a strange plant in a reference.

Because so many wild species wilt quickly in the hand, a camera may provide the best means of taking a "sample" home for further study. Usually, I simply make a sketch in my notebook.

If you are tempted to take wild flowers for replanting at home, you should first check the laws; then study the problems. Hardy as they may seem in their native soil, many wild flowers are extremely sensitive to changes in the amount of shade, soil chemistry and moisture. Most libraries have reference books on how to identify and care for wild flowers.

This is a fine time to begin flower watching. Campions have just started shining white in the dusk. Hawkweed, blueflag, wood lily, wild rose, vetch, lupine, and many more will soon arrive.

As summer wanes there yet will be bellflowers, mints, vervains, wild cucumber and jewelweed, to name a few. The list is long.

Finally, you probably should know that flower watching can be addictive. I have a friend who left a thriving business to seek a simpler life in the north woods. Instead of celebrating the closing of a big business deal, he now exults in the arbutus he finds creeping through fallen pine needles in the spring.

He has stopped to smell the flowers. He is a happy man.

(06/08/67)

TURTLE TALK

A painted turtle crept from the creek behind our country home, paused warily where blueflag fluttered. Then, as its shell dried and dulled, it hastened toward the hill.

The turtle scurried under dogwood and holly bush, where swelling green fruits already followed snowy blossoms. Haltingly then, it crawled through plumes of horsetails, where vetch and wild mints bloomed. It passed withering columbines and wilted trilliums, stained with age. A Mayapple petal fell on the turtle's domed carapace and was held there by a drop of dew.

Beneath arching solomon seals and flowering cranesbills the turtle traveled. With surprising agility, it clambered atop a fallen log, rather than detour from its route. It tumbled over, landing with its plastron shining orange and yellow in the shady woods. Quickly, it righted itself with a flip of extended head, tail and legs. It waited then, alert and very still, in instinctive fear that it had been seen.

And, of course it had. The dog and I had been quietly watching its progress.

The dog must have moved, for the turtle shrank into its shell.

"Mrs. Turtle," I said (for I sometimes talk to turtles). "We give you safe passage. Go on about your business."

And, after posing for a picture, she did.

Her convex undershell had confirmed that the turtle was a female, but her mission had been apparent from the start. It was time for female turtles to seek sunny uplands , where warm earth will incubate their eggs.

It is time too, when spotted fawns lie hidden in sun-dabbled woodlands; when bluebirds, having rested briefly after early broods took wing, begin to nest anew.

Clues, those, that spring has played its part; that summer waits in the wings. And already the scene seems set for a grand finale in the fall. Even now, the hickories and wild cherries show promise of a bountiful harvest. Oak twigs are bulging with buttons of acorns.

The land is lush, full of life. And filled with peril too. Especially for the young.

The slender weasel has grown plump on a bountiful supply of young cottontails and chipmunks this spring. Until it was discovered hunting chipmunks in a woodpile the other day, only its tracks and evidence of its kills had told of its presence around our place.

Trapped between the dog and me, the weasel boldly (and wisely) popped out of my side of the woodpile, studied me coolly for a moment; then streaked for the marsh with the dog in pursuit. So now the hunter also knows the fear of being hunted.

But the turtle was unmindful of all such things. She would do her utmost to hide her eggs from roaming skunks and raccoons. Then she would return to the creek.

She has played her role. The stage is set for the next act. Summer.

(06/16/69)

THE ROAD SHOW

June travelers in Wisconsin are treated to displays as striking in their way as are the breathtaking blush of Door County's cherry trees in spring and the painted woods of the north in fall.

Roadside flowers, including some of the brightest blooms of the year, appear in profusion along state roads as summer nears. Even at highway speeds, a motorist cannot miss the gaudy swirls and blurs of color which rival the boldest works of surrealist painters.

Along many routes, phlox and dame's rockets, ranging from white to deep lavender, are now the showiest roadside blooms. Beside them the wild geranium or cranesbill may appear as dabs of pastel purple. (Cranesbills bloom more profusely, and have deeper hue, where trees shade the bordering woods).

Most colorful is the fiery red-orange of the common hawkweed, mixed at times with the flickering gleam of yellow hawkweed. In the central sand counties they often share the stage with purple lupines, successors to the eye-arresting displays of violets which earlier adorned the same roadside slopes.

In other places the hawkweeds now share sunbeams with spiderworts, The deep, dazzling blue of that species appears as broad swaths of color on the banks and median strip of I-94 between Wisconsin Dells and Mauston. Common too, are the pale yellow blooms of goatsbeards, which wave to morning travelers but close later in the day.

Yarrow and campion are now shining white along highways and byways, and there are places where daisy fleabanes have spread like white sheets across green fields.

Where the road crosses lowlands, as near Millston in Jackson County, the wild iris or blueflag is conspicuous. Glimpses of feathery purple flowers tell that blazing stars or gayfeathers are appearing too.

Those scattered bunches of orange are patches of puccoon, and neighboring swatches of deep purple are vetch, the most prominent plant in the blue spectrum in the north-central counties these days.

Tints of rusty red are being painted by sheep sorrel or dock on many roadsides and hillsides. It is the male plant which has tiny red flowers. Also known as sour grass, the leaves have a puckery taste which is not unpleasant.

(Another ready-made salad can be found in the vinegary, clover-like leaves of the woodsorrel. Its yellow flowers are also blooming, but are too small and scattered to be seen from a car).

The clovers, purple and yellow, carpet many slopes and ditch banks with patterns of color. And the fresh pink petals of wild roses are appearing everywhere, signaling summer's imminent arrival almost everywhere in Wisconsin.

There are others, but these are the ones most often seen by motorists in June. Singly and in concert, they put on quite a show.

Although they are periodically mowed, burned, and soaked with salty run-off from icy roads, most are hardy perennials which bravely, brightly bloom with no helping hand from man.

Slow down sometime. Take a side road. Stroll a while in those untended gardens and meet those streaks of color face to face.

For now you know their names.

(06/19/69)

A WARM WELCOME

Blueflag banners waving in the breeze. Torches of hawkweeds burning along the road. Crowds of pink faces watching from fence rows where wild roses grow. A confetti of butterflies fluttering in the wind. Summer got a warm welcome today.

Nature needs no clock or calendar to know when summer has come, but for us, seasonal changes are calculated by astronomers. Spring ends when our end of this wobbly world tips farthest toward the sun. It is the summer solstice -- our longest day.

Summer will stay until day and night stand equal watches -- the fall equinox. That is only three months hence. Little enough time to take in all of summer's wonders.

The season is a kaleidoscope of color; a marvel of scents and sounds. It is the texture of wool grass, of thistle, of fern and water lily. It is a mist of meadow rue and a crystal pool cupped in a pitcher plant. It is ripening strawberries hiding beneath their leaves, Solomon seals blooming in shady woods, campion stems frothy from spittlebugs; the winking glow of fireflies and the flashing of lightning.

It is also the hum of insects and the rumble of thunder, the quick tempo of an ovenbird's song, the reedy call of the snipe; the piping flute of the wood thrush.

Yet even more than being seen or heard, summer is felt. It draws hard on life, urging, testing; hurrying on. It tempts the young bird to try its wings, but does not pity if it fails. It paints vervains and vetches; then wilts them down. Brush and palette move through woods and field, marsh and meadow, seldom lingering long.

It is a time of ripening berries and falling seeds, fish finning in the tepid current of a thirsty river, the rustle of dragonfly's wings; mouthless Mayflies emerging to their first, and last, day of adult life.

Welcome summer. And then keep moving. The days are long, but time is short.

For summer is the sum of many things.

(06/21/64)

CERTAIN SIGNS

Fireflies flickering across the creek; bullfrog strumming along the moonlit bank...

It seems somewhat familiar.

Sunny goatsbeard blossoms rising to greet the day; white campions shining in fallow fields...

Memories are stirring.

Tree swallows swooping at passersby; muted chatterings of hen teal in the cattails...

Now the pieces are beginning to fit; the picture emerges:

Summer, is that you?

The answer comes from the wild ones, like the swallow whose nest is near our garden. For weeks that bird has been tolerant, even friendly. Now raspy warnings and threatening aerobatics tell that the noisy fledglings are ready to spread their wings. To make sure that the coast is clear for their first, faltering flights, Dad has gone on the attack.

Meanwhile, where blueflags bloom at the water's edge, the teal is lecturing about smartweeds, snails and snapping turtles. Like the mallard and the wood duck, she has a big brood in tow. Late insect hatches meant hard times for the swallow, but our cool, wet spring was just ducky for the teal.

Summer means heightened hazards for the ducklings. Warming water quickens the metabolic rates -- and appetites -- of voracious fish and lurking turtles.

In defense, the duck, ever alert, demands immediate obedience.

"Hide!" she quacks, and her ducklings disappear amid the reeds. "Silence!" and there is not a peep. "Dive!" and there are a dozen swirls. Then feigning a lame wing, she flaps and splashes, luring the danger away.

Nowhere is the discipline and trust between duck and duckling more evident than when the wood duck calls her young from the nest. Wood ducks nest in trees, so every duckling must take to the air long before it has flight feathers.

I have watched their exodus from a hollow in an oak, some 12 feet from the ground. As their mother called below, 15 dark, downy ducklings emerged one by one, to make what appeared to be death-defying leaps. After landing with a bounce on the leafy forest floor, each rallied around their mother. Then, determining that all were present, she marched them off to the creek.

Some wood duck broods are bigger. And some nests are much higher.

Ducks aren't the only busy birds these days. Even the brown thrasher, most exuberant of songsters, has shortened his dawn serenades. Gathering food for growing broods is a dawn to dark task.

Still living in ease, however, are the cowbirds (which simply leave their eggs for adoption in other nests) and the goldfinches, which have not yet nested.

One would think that the goldfinch, having wintered with us, would have a head start on the migrants which return to breed in spring. Instead, goldfinches wait until midsummer when there will be thistledown to line their nests. Then too, they will have succulent seeds to feed their young. Milkweed seeds, already "chewed" by the parents, are favorites of little finches.

There are more birds this year. In addition to such colorful songsters as orioles, cardinals and rosebreasted grosbeaks -- all perennial residents -- we've been seeing scarlet tanagers. And, while redbellied, downy and hairy woodpeckers are common callers, this is only the second summer in 15 years that our woods have hosted redheaded woodpeckers.

Calls of the towhee, wood thrush, veery and ovenbird also are other familiar sounds these days, but one thing has been missing. For years we had two or more pairs of bluebirds nesting around our place, and each usually raised two broods before departing with autumn's final flashes of color. The sight and sound of them was always a joy. Moreover, no beetle had much chance of survival while our garden was under their watchful eyes. Then, last year there were none.

Similar reports were widespread. Sometime between the autumn of 1977 and spring of 1988, some unknown disaster befell the eastern bluebird population.

This spring their favorite house was again kept closed to sparrows and swallows, but May arrived and left with no sign of those songsters which wear the colors of summer skies, glowing sunsets and cottony clouds.

Then, just this week, while working in the yard, I thought I heard a flight song in the distance. I stopped, straining eyes and ears, but I needn't have. A cock bluebird fluttered down to our weathervane, perched there and broke into song. I felt like doing the same.

Wild roses, which usually blossom as summer arrives, are still barely budded around our place. Juneberries are ripening late, and columbines are lingering uncommonly long in the shaded woods.

But though her approach was stormy and her manner cool, that was summer coming up the path all right.

A little bird told me so.

(06/22/79)

SUDDENLY IT'S SUMMER

Wild roses beaming from a fencerow. A veery's song spiraling from the woods at dawn. A whippoorwill lilting to the moon.

So suddenly, it's summer.

One wonders, sometimes, if summer will ever find its way through an uncertain spring. It was mid-March this year when winter fled before a rush of wings. By mid-April the migrations appeared to be three weeks ahead of schedule. But then in May, spring lost all of those gains and more. Frost gnawed at bud and blossom.

June had a lot of catching up to do if it was to bring summer in on cue. She has done so in a fast-stepping parade, with great bursts of color and music. There have been huge bouquets of scarlet and gold columbines, magenta cranesbills, blue violets and vetch. Shooting stars have showered the forest with pastel blossoms as the trilliums faded.

Choruses of birdsong were led by the pipings of the wood thrush and arias from the brown thrasher.

There was a day when the woods were strewn with honeysuckle petals; another when holly blossoms swirled like a blizzard around the tamarack swamp. Could summer be late for such a celebration?

The answer is easy to find these days when the sun rises in a red haze; these nights when fireflies flicker across the fields.

Empty rabbit nests -- faint hollows lined with soft fur -- reveal that the cottontail's perennial population explosion is well begun. Speckle-bellied robins, downy ducklings and half-pint chipmunks tell of other empty nests.

On a sandy knoll near the creek, another nest was emptied by a nocturnal raider. There a skunk or raccoon has sniffed out a cache of eggs buried by a turtle. However, having left incubation to the sun and the nest to fate, the turtle does not mourn the loss.

Come autumn, the raccoons will glut on wild grapes near the raided nest. Hardbitten by frost in May, the tangled vines have flowered anew. For foragers, it looks like a good year after all.

Nature is back on schedule. Hawkweeds blaze like tiny sunbursts along the path. Bees are bumbling in clover-scented fields. Green cattail spikes are swelling in the marsh. But there is much more to be done. Those seemingly sleepy, humdrum summer days are really times of great activity and change.

Spring, you see, makes promises only summer can keep.

(06/23/83)

BACK ON SCHEDULE

Golden goatsbeard blossoms are opening like sunbursts in the fields. A froth of tiny bedstraw blossoms is bordering the marsh. Feathery flowers have appeared on grey dogwoods and brown-eyed susans are waving cheerily along the creek bank.

So, summer has sauntered into our little neck of the woods just about on schedule, despite delays caused by dalliances of spring.

Of course, if you judge by the calendar or chronometer, summer is always here right on the dot. It arrives at that moment when the sun halts its journey northward. Then, having delivered the year's longest day, it heads southward to fetch us another winter.

But summer is something more that. It is a sum of sounds and scents and small events which, although appearing haphazard, occur with surprisingly precise timing and patterns. The procession of wildflowers, for example, is always the same. In our woods it begins with bloodroots, sometimes braving snow, and it ends with huddled gentians and frosted asters in the marsh. And each arrives with timing which sometimes seems uncanny.

Wild roses herald summer's arrival in our latitudes, and they seldom miss the calendar date by more than a couple of days. And although an uncommonly cold spring, plus weeks of drought, have delayed the corn I planted, the shadbush and columbines started blooming right on time.

Neither do the birds require clocks or calendars to keep them on schedule. A robin's nest, already empty, hangs in tatters from a recent storm. In a nearby cedar, another nest is overflowing with four fledgling bluejays. Hungry choruses sound from the swallow houses, and concerned swoopings of the parents tell us that the young are ready to try their wings.

Now too, tiny turtles, hatched in warm earth, crawl unerringly toward the creek they've never seen. Now bees bumble and toads trill and catbirds mew to dazzling afternoons.

Juneberries and redosier fruits are already ripening, while wild grapes, still no bigger than BB shots, show promise of a bumper crop to gladden the raccoons.

Yellow hawkweed, purple nightshade, pale pink rose. Brown thrashers singing sweetly to the dawns. Fireflies flashing through the nights. All add up to an announcement:

It is time to celebrate with picnics and parties on the patio.

Summer is here for sure.

06/24/78

JUNE DAYS, JUNE NIGHTS

"And what is so rare as a day in June,?" asked the poet James Russell Lowell in 1848.

He waited around quite a while for an answer, dying in Cambridge. Mass., in August, 1891, after a distinguished career as a man of letters, a professor at Harvard and an ambassador to Europe.

So there the question has rested. Except that is arises anew with the reveille of birds these gentle dawns.

It is whispered when the first stirrings of day carry the scent of sweet clover, when dew-laden fields sparkle at sunrise; when deep pink wild roses blush on the hills.

The spaniel revels in the tall, wet clover. Tiny yellow petals cling to his coat as we make our morning rounds. Here and there, in fields of gold, is the startling blue of spiderworts; the striking purple of thistles.

A rosebreasted grosbeak tunes up in the woods. An oriole answers from nearby; a cardinal from afar. But their voices are muted now, and fewer than in spring. June is far to busy a time for birds to dally and serenade.

The bluejays are silent now. Meadowlarks speak in chattering notes, their cheery whistles seldom heard. The bobolink, bluebird and thrasher seem strangely subdued. The redwings that thronged in the marsh not long ago now act secretive.

"J-rrrrr-UP!" A tree swallow reveals his secret with a threatening call as he swoops at my head. The swallows nested in a bluebird house at the edge of our garden, and, until now, that natty fellow and his mate regarded intruders only with curiosity. Now though, his actions tell of young in the nest. A peek reveals an array of bright eyes and expectant beaks.

Meanwhile, a brood of bluebirds call hungrily from another house near the dog kennel. More tolerant, their parents pay little heed to our passings. However, that will change one day soon. When their fledglings are ready to venture into the world, even the bluebirds will press frenzied attacks against man, dog, chipmunk, grackle, and every threatening shadow. They will not rest until the young have found the wonder of their wings.

Young squirrels are scrambling in the trees. Shards of shells from hidden stores tell that their clan is still feasting on last fall's bounty of hickory nuts.

Goatsbeard blossoms have seeded to airy spheres amid bright new faces of brown eyed susans and snowy drifts of cress and campion. A goldfinch, perhaps impatient for thistledown to line its tiny nest, tugs at the goatsbeard's silken plumes.

In the creek sunfish sleep, open eyed, awakening to the tiniest dimpling of a fallen bug. Now even the mosquito has lost its shrillness. It alights lazily in the grass as the sun steams the dew away.

Priceless days these, truly deserving the celebration of poets.

"June may be had by the poorest comer," Lowell noted.

But then there are sunsets tinted with all of summer's hues, and velvet darkness with fireflies rising like sparks of foxfire, and stars crowding close to earth. We can hear frogs strumming and owl talk, and the birdlike conversations of young raccoons discussing new discoveries.

The answer to the poet's question seems easy then:

June days may be rare indeed, but a June night is rarer still.

(06/26/76)